DATE DUE

LANGUAGES, TERRITORIES, AND NAMES OF CALIFORNIA INDIAN TRIBES

ROBERT F. HEIZER

LANGUAGES TERRITORIES AND NAMES OF CALIFORNIA INDIAN TRIBES

UNIVERSITY OF CALIFORNIA PRESS
BERKELEY AND LOS ANGELES

UNIVERSITY OF CALIFORNIA PRESS
BERKELEY AND LOS ANGELES, CALIFORNIA

CAMBRIDGE UNIVERSITY PRESS
LONDON, ENGLAND

LIBRARY OF CONGRESS CATALOG CARD NUMBER 66-25615
PRINTED IN THE UNITED STATES OF AMERICA

ACKNOWLEDGMENTS

The present work was prepared under an agreement with the Smithsonian Institution. I wish to acknowledge the help of Dr. S. Dillon Ripley, Secretary of the Smithsonian Institution, who authorized a grant from the E. H. Harriman Fund for the purpose of preparing the linguistic stock and tribal distribution map based on Dr. C. Hart Merriam's data files, which have been, since 1950, deposited in the Department of Anthropology, University of California, Berkeley.

Also deserving mention, with my thanks, are Mrs. A. L. Kroeber, Mrs. Edna Flood, Miss Linda Handjian, Miss Caroline Hills, Mr. Robert Berner, and Mr. Jay C. von Werlhof, who aided me in various ways.

CONTENTS

Maps

INTRODUCTION

The Indians of California first became known to Europeans in 1542, 50 years after the discovery of America by Columbus. The earliest written eyewitness description of California Indians (mainly the Chumash peoples of the Santa Barbara region), their culture, and a record of the names of villages in which they lived dates from the expedition of Cabrillo in 1542 (Wagner, 1928). The voyage of Vizcaino in 1602 adds a bit more of this kind of information, as do the slightly earlier records of the California visits in 1579 of Francis Drake (Wagner, 1926; Taylor, 1932; Heizer, 1947; Heizer and Elmendorf, 1942), and the account of the Indians at Drake's Bay in 1595 by Cermeno (Wagner, 1924; Heizer, 1942). In their totality there is very little of ethnological significance in these early expeditionary journals. When the Spaniards decided to enter California by land expeditions setting out from Mexico, as they did in 1769, there was more intimate contact with the Indians, with the result that somewhat fuller descriptions of native culture and the people themselves were recorded. While the Spaniards were always interested in the Indians, they did not study them and record the details of their way of life, customs, and languages because these facts were considered unimportant as contributing to the knowledge of mankind (see Cutter, 1960). Indeed, with a very limited number of exceptions, there was no systematic investigation and recording of the culture of the California Indians in the Spanish period. The most notable exception is the document compiled between 1812 and 1826 by Fr. Geronimo Boscana concerning the religion of the Indians of the Mission of San Juan Capistrano (Kroeber, 1959). A more general ethnographic document, dating from 1811 and published in abbreviated form by Kroeber (1908*b*) and more fully, though not completely, by Geiger (1949, 1950), is in the form of a schedule or questionnaire, consisting of 35 questions which were answered in writing by priests attached to the Franciscan missions in California. A third important Spanish document is the linguistic study performed by Padre Arroyo de la Cuesta about 1821. A few portions of it have been published, but the whole work still awaits publication. During the whole of the Spanish-Mexican period of California history, from 1542 to 1850, no person attempted to write a general ethnographic sketch of the California Indians who were known, or to place the names and locations of known tribal groups on a map of the territory. There is nothing surprising about this, but the fact is of interest.

TYPES OF TRIBAL ORGANIZATION

One way to begin the systematic study of the groups and cultures of a large area is to ascertain the names of the groups and the territories which they occupied. All peoples are, to varying degrees, bound to the land on which they live and from which they derive their livelihood. Some peoples cling tenaciously to one area which is their traditional home, and which provides them with the materials to make their houses, clothing, tools and utensils, as well as with the food they need for survival. Other peoples are less consciously land-owning and territorially bound, and may move at will over a large area where local group ownership is minimal or even lacking.

In native California the sedentary pattern is illustrated by the Yurok tribe of Humboldt County in the northwestern part of the state, where the particular type of culture operated to prevent the formation of a strong, unified tribal organization. This can be illustrated by two quotations from A. L. Kroeber (1925:3, 14):

Property and rights pertain to the realm of the individual, and the Yurok recognizes no public claim and the existence of no community. His world is wholly an aggregation of individuals. There being no society as such, there is no social organization. Clans, exogamic groups, chiefs or governors, political units, are unrepresented even by traces in northwestern California. The germinal, nameless political community that can be traced among the Indians of the greater part of the State is absent. Government being wanting, there is no authority, and without authority there can be no chief. The men so called are individuals whose wealth, and their ability to retain and employ it, have clustered about them an aggregation of kinsmen, followers, and semidependents to whom they dispense assistance and protection. If a man usually marries outside the village in which he lives, the reason is that many of his coinhabitants normally happen to be blood relatives, not because custom or morality recognize the village as a unit concerned with marriage. The actual outcome among the Yurok may, in the majority of cases, be the same as among nations consciously organized on an exogamic plan. The point of view, the guiding principles both of the individual's action and of the shaping of the civilization, are wholly nonexogamic. Such familiar terms as "tribe," "village community," "chief," "government," "clan," can therefore be used with reference to the Yurok only after extreme care in previous definition – in their current senses they are wholly inapplicable.

It is essential to bear in mind that since there was no definite community sense within a village, there was no opportunity for a larger or political community to develop out of a group of adjacent villages. One settlement in such a group – a "suburb" – was sometimes involved in a feud while another directly across the river looked on. Of course, wherever kinship existed, it formed a definite bond between towns as within them; but however instrumental blood relationship may sometimes become as a means of political organization, it is not in itself productive of a political sense; and the replacement of the latter by a feeling of kinship or personal relation among people like the Yurok is precisely what makes it necessary to distinguish the two if this peculiar society is to be understood.

A significantly reduced sense of attachment of persons to specific localities is illustrated by the Mohave tribe, which lived on the Colorado River. Of them Kroeber (1925:727) wrote:

For every people hitherto mentioned in this book a list of towns or villages has had some significance. When such information has not been given ignorance has been the sole cause. The settlement is the political and social basis of life in California. The tribe, at least as a larger unit, exists hardly or not at all. The reverse is the case with the Mohave. They think also of their land as a country, and of its numberless places. They do not think of its settlements. Where a man is born or lives is like the circumstance of a street number among ourselves, not part of the fabric of his career. The man stands in relation to the group as a whole, and this group owns a certain tract rich in associations; but the village does not enter into the scheme. In fact, the Mohave were the opposite of clannish in their inclinations. Their settlements were small, scattering, and perhaps often occupied only for short times; the people all mixed freely with one another.

With such proclivities, it is small wonder that the petty Californian feuds of locality and inherited revenge have given way among the Mohave to a military spirit, under which the tribe acted as a unit in offensive and defensive enterprise. Tribes hundreds of miles away were attacked and raided. Visits carried parties of Mohave as far as the Chumash and Yokuts. Sheer curiosity was their main motive; for the Mohave were little interested in trade. They liked to see lands; timidity did not discourage them; and they were as eager to know the manners of other peoples as they were careful to hold aloof from adopting them.

A somewhat different situation regarding the nature of the tribe as an organization holds for the 50 or so Yokuts tribes of the San Joaquin Valley area, of whom Kroeber (1925:474) writes:

The Yokuts are unique among the California natives in one respect. They are divided into true tribes. Each has a name, a dialect, and a territory. The first of these traits, the group name, is wanting in other Californians, who normally are able to designate themselves only by the appellation of the place they inhabit. The second feature, dialectic separateness, of course is an old story for California, but elsewhere in the State each idiom is usually common to a considerable number of tribelets or "village communities." Only in the third trait, their political independence and their ownership of a tract of land, are the ordinary Californian village communities and the Yokuts tribes similar.

Forty of these tribes are sufficiently known to be locatable. In the northern part of the Yokuts areas the map is, however, blank except for a few names of groups of uncertain situation and doubtful affinities. The total number of tribes may therefore have reached fifty. Such an array of dialects is unparalleled, and gives to the Yokuts alone nearly one-third of all the different forms of speech talked in the State. The differences of language from tribe to tribe were often rather limited; but they are marked enough to be readily perceptible to the interested Caucasian observer. Since the total length of the Yokuts area does not much exceed 250 miles and the breadth nowhere attains to 100, the individual geographical range of these little languages was exceedingly narrow. Their territory averaged perhaps 300 square miles — say a half day's foot journey in each direction from the center.

Some of the tribes occupied a single spot with sufficient permanence to become identified with it: thus the Wowol on Atwells Island in Tulare Lake, the Gawia and Yokod on opposite sides of Kaweah River where this leaves the hills, the Choinimni at the junction of Mill Creek and Kings River. Such groups, save for their distinctive speech, would be indistinguishable from the village communities of their neighbors if the purely local designations of the latter were replaced by appellations for the people themselves. Still fainter is the line of demarcation when the Choinimni, for instance, are called, as occasionally happens, Tishechuchi after their town Tishechu; but such terms are rare among the Yokuts.

For other tribes a principal and several subsidiary abodes are specified; thus the Paleuyami are identified with Altau and sometimes called Altinin, but lived also at Bekiu, Shikidapau, Holmiu, and other places. The Hometwoli lived at three principal sites, and the Chukchansi, Tachi, Yauelmani, and others dwelt from time to time, and perhaps simultaneously, at a number of places scattered over a considerable tract. These instances confirm the Yokuts divisions as true tribes.

Fully half the Yokuts tribal names end either in -amni, found also as -imni, -mina, -mani; or in -chi. The former suffix recurs added to place names among the Plains Miwok to designate the inhabitants of such and such spots, and among the Maidu as an ending of village names; the latter among the southern Miwok with the significance "people of." But the subtraction of either of these endings from the names of Yokuts tribes usually leaves only meaningless syllables; and in general the people themselves are well content to employ their little national designations without inquiring what they may denote.

The tribelet or "village community" type of organization is described by Kroeber (1932:257-259) as follows:

It has gradually become clear that in the region west and northwest of the Patwin there prevailed a type of political organization which has been veiled by the shrinkage, removal, and amalgamation of the natives in recent generations, by the fact that the units were small and often nameless, that they frequently lived in several settlements, and that each settlement has a recognized headman who, as well as the group head, was called chief. Barrett [1908] was the first to bring out the relation of the settlement and subchief to the group as a whole and its chief, for some of the Yuki. His Pomo geographical studies revealed such a number of inhabited sites as to make it evident that these were not all politically equivalent and independent units. Had they been such, the Pomo population would have had to be estimated at 25,000 or more. On the basis of data in his monograph, in Powers, and in earlier statements, and with reference to the topography, I therefore mapped some seventy-five Pomo groups; those in the north with relative assurance, in the south tentatively. Each of these seemed to possess a small territory usually definable in terms of drainage; a principal town or settlement, often with a chief recognized by the whole group; normally, minor settlements which might or might not be occupied permanently; and sometimes a specific name, but more often none other than the designation of the principal town. Each group acted as a homogeneous unit in matters of land ownership, trespass, war, major ceremonies, and the entertainment entailed by them. The average population I estimated at not far from a hundred souls per unit. This figure may be somewhat low, since prosperous groups reached two or three hundred. For the Clear Lake Pomo, Gifford [1923] has since confirmed the conjectured tribal delimitations through field inquiries and has added many illuminating details, such as the fact that a unit might be headed by two or three chiefs, each recognized by the individuals in the community related to him by blood.

Goddard in two recent papers on the Wailaki, based partly on data secured before 1909, has brought out a similar type of organization. He calls the units "sub-tribes" with reference to all the Wailaki as a "tribe," but this is merely a difference in nomenclature.

On the other side of the Patwin there are some indications that the Maidu were organized in the same way, at any rate in the mountains; and more recently Gifford has found the Central Sierra Miwok of the upper foothills to possess not only units of somewhat similar type but a name for them, nana. These Miwok units seem to have been somewhat smaller territorially and numerically, perhaps on account of the food supply or topography, the larger streams not being habitable in this area. The Yokuts and Western Mono have long been known to be divided into definite tribes, which however differed from those north of them in possessing names for themselves, speaking at least slightly distinct dialects, and averaging a population of several hundred souls.

It is thus evident that in much of central California there prevailed a type of political organization into what may be called "tribelets"; groups of small size, definitely owning a restricted territory, nameless except for their tract or its best known spot, speaking usually a dialect identical with that of several of their neighbors, but wholly autonomous. This more definite concept must replace the vaguer one of the "village" or "village community." If the tribelet was concentrated in one settlement, as among the Clear Lake Pomo, the village and the tribelet happened to coincide. But as Barrett's and Goddard's maps show, this was most frequently not the case, especially in hill country. Usually, therefore, the village was but an incident in the history and consciousness of the tribelet. The latter was the functioning unit.

One of the main aims of anthropological inquiry in studies of California Indian cultures of the past half-century has been to determine what the extent and boundaries of tribal territories were, as well as to learn what techniques were employed by the occupants to gain a livelihood from those areas which they occupied. The result of two programs of this kind of investigation, expressed in the form of maps of California showing tribal territories, one by Professor Alfred L. Kroeber of the University of California, and the other by Dr. C. Hart Merriam, Research Associate of the Smithsonian Institution, are presented here.

The student who looks at the map may wonder why tribal territories do not conform more closely with natural physiographic divisions. An excellent discussion of the relations of aboriginal cultures to environment in California is found in Jones (1951). Kroeber (1908*c*:283) discussed this matter as follows:

It is still sometimes thought that areas of diverse native languages can be pretty closely correlated in California with areas that are physiographically distinct. Nothing is more erroneous. True, as there are so many forms of speech, the great majority of them can extend over only a small territory, and it is only natural that a small territory should often be confined entirely to a certain physiographical area. But there are numerous instances where not only linguistic families, but even dialects, run counter to all natural boundaries. The Shoshoneans and Washo have both spilled over the high crest of the Sierra Nevada. The Pomo west of the main Coast Range have an offshoot in the Sacramento valley, and the Wintun of this valley occupy territory west of the Coast Range. The Yurok are in part an ocean people, like their neighbors the Wiyot, and in part a river people on the same stream as their neighbors the Karok. Shoshonean people lived in the timbered Sierra, in the Great Basin drainage, the hot deserts of the interior of southern California, the fertile parts of the coast region of southern California, and shared the Santa Barbara islands with the Chumash. The southern Maidu dialect was spoken in the Sacramento valley plains, in the foothills, and in the high Sierra. The northern and central Pomo dialects were each spoken on the immediate coast, in the open Russian river valley, and in the intervening heavily timbered mountainous redwood belt. In certain instances where languages or dialects correspond to physiographic areas, these physiographic areas lack any separating barrier. Thus among the Yokuts and Miwok the dialects of the level plain of the San Joaquin valley are with scarcely an exception quite sharply distinct from the dialects of the adjacent foothill country

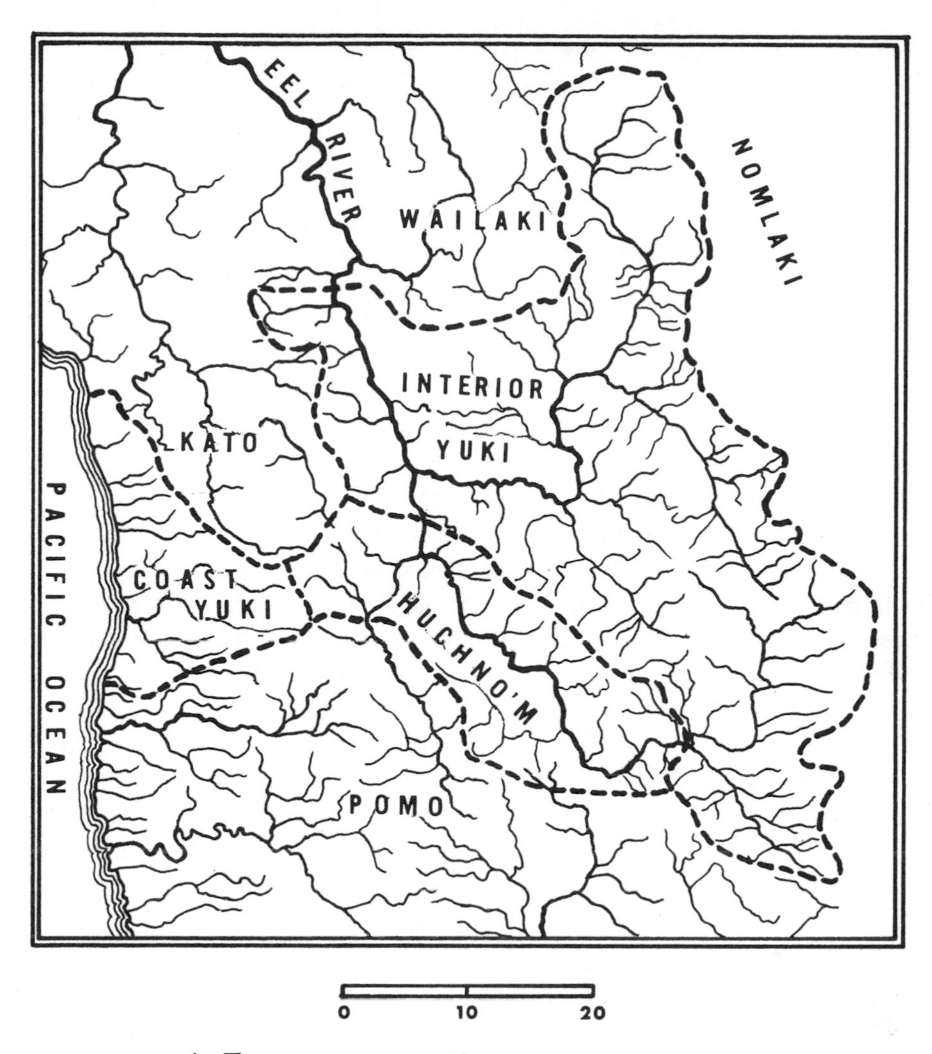

MAP 1. TERRITORY OF THE YUKI (FROM KROEBER, 1925).

of the Sierra; and yet the change from plain to hills is so gradual in some parts as to be scarcely visible. It is clear that in such cases the direct cause of the difference of speech is not the environment itself, but a difference in association and mode of life dependent upon physical geography. In fact it is even going too far to name these dialectic divergences as effects and other factors as causes; we are really only justified in saying that the differentiation of speech seems to be causally related with other factors, and that these are immediately cultural and historical, and only indirectly physical and environmental.

Lest the occupancy of territory seems, from the above quotation, to have been totally without system of plan, we add another quotation from Kroeber

(1925:160-161) on the importance of drainage areas as determinants of tribal domains:

> As seen on the map [Map 1], the distribution of the Yuki seems irregular. This is not because their location ran counter to natural topography but because it followed it. Their country lies wholly in the Coast Range mountains, which in this region are not, on the whole, very high, but are much broken. They contain some valleys, but the surface of the land in general is endlessly rugged. The Yuki habitat is, however, not defined, except incidentally, by limiting mountains and ranges, but is given in block by the drainage of such-and-such streams. The native did not think, like a modern civilized man, of his people owning an area circumscribed by a definite line, in which there might happen to be one or many watercourses. This would have been viewing the land through a map, whether drawn or mental; and such an attitude was foreign to his habit. What he did know was that the little town at which he was born and where he expected to die lay on a certain river or branch of a river; and that this stream, or a certain stretch of it, and all the creeks flowing into it, and all the land on or between these creeks, belonged to his people; whereas below, or above, or across certain hills, were other streams and tributaries, where other people lived, with whom he might be on visiting terms or intermarried, but who had proprietary rights of their own.
>
> Yuki territory may be described as all the land lying in the drainage of Eel River above the North Fork, except for a stretch on South Eel River where the allied Huchnom were situated. This sounds and is simple enough. It is nature's fault, and not any intricacy of the Yuki mind or subtlety of Yuki institutions, if this extraordinarily compact and unitary fact takes form on our maps in the shape of a meaninglessly curved, indented, and irregular border.

The general principle that drainage areas marked by crests or watersheds, rather than main stream courses themselves, act as boundary lines has been found to be generally true of North American Indians. The tribal distribution map of North America prepared by Kroeber (1939) illustrates this phenomenon.

IDENTIFICATION AND CLASSIFICATION OF TRIBAL GROUPS

The main tribal units are identified on the basis of the languages which they spoke. The tribal map is, therefore, essentially a linguistic map. Within the geographically bounded major-language units, it is possible to establish subdivisions, which are based upon speech dialects, or politically separate units. Kroeber (1925: 3, 160-163, 228-230, 234-235, 474-475, 727) has discussed the nature of the tribe among California Indians, as well as the nature of the land-holding groups in aboriginal California (see also Kroeber, 1962). He concluded that the "tribelet" was the basic political and social unit in native California in that it was "self-governing, independent, and land-owning" (Kroeber, 1955*b*; 1962:37). For some California tribes, to which Kroeber (1936:73-74; 1951:119; 1962) refers to by the alternative term of "ethnic nationalities," there exists fairly full information on the number, names, and territories of the tribelet groups which go to make up the larger linguistic ("tribal") unit; among these are the Achomawi (Merriam, 1926; Kniffen, 1928,) the Pomo (Stewart, 1943), the Yokuts (Kroeber, 1925), and the River Patwin (Kroeber, 1932). But for large parts of the state the data are too fragmentary to enable us to easily identify and locate with any accuracy the tribelet territories. Kroeber (1962:30) estimates that California held between 500 and 600 of these "independent and separate definable groups." It may be anticipated that future scholars, undaunted by the huge mass of available published and manuscript data on California Indians, will work over the information on a tribe-by-tribe basis and prepare maps showing the domains of the identifiable or inferable tribelets. Such a task is far too complex and time-consuming to be attempted here.

THE HISTORY OF LANGUAGE CLASSIFICATION IN CALIFORNIA

Even untrained observers can often distinguish two neighboring languages which are somewhat different, but related, from two neighboring languages which are quite different. The Spanish explorers often made such observations. In 1792, for example, Longinos (1961:57) wrote about the Santa Barbara Channel region: "Although customs vary only slightly in the forty or fifty leagues of this district, there is a great difference in languages. I have observed as many as five. Some of them are fairly alike and the Indians understand each other to a certain extent, but the rest are entirely distinct. The confusion resulting from there being so many languages in such a short distance would make a dictionary of them of little utility for history." The last sentence in this passage shows that classification of languages for its own sake was considered useless. Arroyo de la Cuesta in 1821 made a series of careful linguistic records, in the form of word lists, phrases, and grammatical forms, of a number of mission Indian languages, but his work was almost unique for its time. Two of his major studies are published (Arroyo de la Cuesta, 1861, 1862; Mason, 1916), but his great *Idiomas* manuscript has not yet been printed. Paolo Tac, an Indian neophyte attached to Mission San Luis Rey by reason of his birth at that place in 1822, went to Rome from 1834 to 1841 and there recorded a large body of Luiseño linguistic material and ethnography (Hewes, 1952). This has been discussed and cited by Kroeber and Grace (1960, App. I).

It was the practice of exploring expeditions, mainly Spanish, French, and English, in the late eighteenth and early nineteenth centuries, to collect and publish short word and phrase lists of the languages of the native peoples living at places where the ships remained for a period of time (cf. Scouler, 1841; Duflot de Mofras, 1814). For California, and almost exclusively referring to coastal tribes, there are such word lists for the Chumash, Esselen, Salinan, Costanoan, Coast Miwok, Pomo, and Yurok groups. These have all been used, insofar as their crude renderings are utilizable, from the beginning of the American period, when the first serious attempts were made to try to collect all available linguistic information and subject it to comparative analysis. Some of this early effort is summarized by Gallatin and George Gibbs (in Schoolcraft, 1853, Part III:397-460). To this period also belongs the work of Johnston (1854) and Hale (1846). As early as 1854, Latham (see also Turner, 1856:84) was able to prove that Hupa was linked with the Athabascan (i.e., Navajo-Apache) languages of the southwestern United States. Latham (1856:74-87) made what can be called the first real attempt at classifying California Indian languages. He lists the following "groups": Lutuami, Paliak and Shasta (of Oregon and California); Ehnik (i.e., Karok), Tahlewah (i.e., Tolowa); languages akin to the Weitspek (Wiyot and Wishosk); Mendocino (?) group (i.e., Pomo and [?] Yuki); Copeh (i.e., Patwin); Pujuni (i.e., Maidu); Moquelumne group (i.e., Miwok); Costano (i.e., Costanoan); Mariposa languages (i.e., Yokuts); Salinas group (i.e., Yokuts and/or Southern Sierra Miwok); Santa Barbara group (i.e., Chumash); Capistrano group (i.e., Shoshonean represented by Luiseño, Gabrielino, Fernandeño, and Juaneño) and Yuma (i.e., Diegueño, Yuma). It will be noted that many of Latham's names have survived, having been accepted by Powell (1891) and later by Dixon and Kroeber (1919). An indefatigable field collector and reprinter of California Indian vocabularies was Alexander S. Taylor, whose famous series of articles entitled "Indianology of California" appeared in the newspaper, *California Farmer and Journal of Useful Sciences* (Taylor, 1860-1863). Taylor did not make any special effort to point out linguistic relationships, presumably for the reason that he was more interested in printing facts than in analyzing them. The Shoshonean or Uto-Aztekan family was early recognized (Kroeber, 1904; Lamb, 1964), and later work served to identify and add to the list of languages which belonged to this family.

In the 1870's there came a great spurt of new activities in this field. The Wheeler Survey West of the One Hundredth Meridian, performed at the instigation of the War Department, was instructed to carry out ethnological and archaeological investigations, and part of this work consisted of collecting linguistic information in the form of words and phrases. Most of this information was collected by Oscar Loew in 1875, and there appeared a preliminary analysis of 11 of the word lists by Gatschet (1876*a*), who concluded that three "distinct Families of aboriginal languages" were represented, these being labelled Santa Barbara, Shoshonee, and Yuma. In the same year Gatschet (1876*b*) published an analysis of 12 languages of southwestern North America and was able to list (pp. 28-33) 42 speech families of North America. Many of these families were by this time known to include a number of dialects, and these are also listed by Gatschet. Gatschet again took up the analysis of the vocabularies collected by the Wheeler Survey specialists and in 1879 published a substantial appendix to Volume VII of the Wheeler Survey Reports, consisting of 40 vocabularies which he subsumed into seven southwestern and Californian stocks (Tinne, Numa, Yuma, Rio Grande Pueblos, Kera Pueblos, Wintun, and Santa Barbara). Gatschet (1877-1886) published data on the Yuman languages and firmly established this speech family. A few years earlier Stephen Powers, a journalist who had travelled among and studied the Indians of California, published his volume entitled *Tribes of California* (Powers, 1877). An appendix to Powers' volume, written by J. W. Powell and entitled *Linguistics,* runs to 174 pages and includes 80 word lists from California. These are drawn from many sources, with the Smithsonian Institution files being well represented. Powell's list of 13 families in which these dialects are classified is reproduced here, along with the number of vocabularies represented:

Karok (5)
Yurok (6)
Chimariko (1)
Wishosk (3)
Yuki (4)
Pomo (11)
Wintun (12)

Mutsun (12)
Santa Barbara (4)
Yokuts (6)
Maidu (8)
Achomawi (2)
Shasta (5)

Powell tentatively classes as a separate language the speech of San Antonio Mission (cf. Sitjar, 1861), which had earlier been classed (incorrectly) by Gatschet (1876*a*) as belonging to the Santa Barbara stock. A major paper by Gatschet in 1877 dealt with languages west of the Rockies. His approach can be judged by the following: "My principal purpose was to give a *correct division* of the idioms into stocks, and their dialects and subdialects." Deriving much of his information from Powers (1877), he lists the following California "stocks": Yuma, Santa Barbara, Mutsun, Yocut, Meewoc, Meidoo, Wintoon, Yuka, Pomo, Wishosk, Eurok, Weitspek, Cahrok, Tolewa, Shasta, Pit River, Klamath, and Hoopa. M. P. de Lucy-Fossarieu (1881) published a series of 22 vocabularies of California Indians, but the work is of no significance since it is mainly a reprinting of already published word lists and no attempt is made at classification. About the same may be said for Chapters IV and V in Hubert H. Bancroft's Volume III of *Native Races of the Pacific States of North America* (1875), where he cites a number of opinions, most of them quite uninformed, on relationships and reproduces a number of short comparative word lists. In 1882 Gatschet resurveyed the accumulated information, but lists only Mutsun, Wintun, Chimariko, and Washo among Californian languages, although he knew of many more. The addition of Washo to the 1877 list may have been stimulated by H. E. Hayden (1877), who called attention to Captain Simpson's report on exploration of the Great Basin, which contained (Collins, 1876) a number of Shoshonean word lists and the statement that the Washoe dialect is different and "not related to the Shoshonee."

In 1878 Alphonse Pinart, together with his companion, Leon de Cessac, were engaged in ethnological and archaeological explorations in California under the auspices of the Musée d'Ethnographie du Trocadero, now called the Musée de l'Homme (Reichlen and Heizer, 1964). Pinart collected a number of vocabularies, 13 of which were published by Heizer (1952). Pinart also wrote a large work entitled *Vocabularios de las Lenguas Indigenas de la Alta California,* which he intended, or hoped, to publish in Paris in 1902. The manuscript, which was not published and which is now in the Yale University Library, consists of copies of several scores of vocabularies drawn, for the most part, from published sources and archives, such as those of the Smithsonian Institution.

At various times between 1880 and 1888 H. W. Henshaw, who had earlier been associated with the Wheeler Survey, visited California to record linguistic materials under the sponsorship of the Bureau of American Ethnology. Among Henshaw's accomplishments was the recognition of the Esselen linguistic family (Henshaw, 1890). Major J. W. Powell, a long-time friend of Henshaw, was the founder of the Bureau and asked Henshaw to work for the Bureau in order to have his assistance in the great work of establishing a classification of the Indian languages of North America. Details of Henshaw's activities in California can be found in Heizer (1955: 85-89), and the complicated relationships between Powell and his aides (Henshaw, Curtin, Gatschet, and Dorsey) in the linguistic classification project are treated by Sturtevant (1959), Kroeber (1960), and Hymes (1961). In 1891 Powell in his monumental *Indian Linguistic Families of America North of Mexico* classified California languages into 22 families.[1] This was reduced to 21 following publication in 1905 of Dixon's demonstration that Shasta and Achomawi, considered separate by Powell, were related. Dixon and Kroeber (1913) had examined regional types of languages in California, but deliberately refrained from attempting at that time to establish language families. In 1912 and 1913, Dixon and Kroeber did go beyond their previous efforts and proposed to reduce the number of linguistic families in California from 21 to 15 that were certainly demonstrable, and perhaps to as few as 12. This reduction was made possible by showing the relationship of the five Penutian languages (Maidu, Wintun, Miwok, Yokuts, and Costanoan), of the three certain Hokan languages (Shasta, Chimariko, and Pomo) and two possible Hokan languages (Karok and Yana), and of the two Ritwan languages (Yurok and Wiyot). Sapir (1913) verified the relationship of Wiyot and Yurok[2] and, in addition, proved that they were both members of the Algonkian linguistic family. A few years later Dixon and Kroeber (1919) published the evidence for a final reduction of California languages to seven families (Penutian, Hokan, Algonkian, Athabascan, Uto-Aztekan, Yukian, and Lutuamian). This is the classification used by Kroeber in his *Handbook of the Indians of California,* which was written in 1918 but not published until 1925.

There is no claim that this brief survey of the history of classification of California native languages is complete, but it does present the essential outline of what took place up to 1919. In the past 50 years a great amount of field work and publication on California Indian languages has been accomplished, but this has not led to any fundamental alteration of the classification arrived at by Dixon and Kroeber in 1919.

For the history of the classification of North American Indian languages the reader may consult the following: Powell (1891), Voegelin (1941),

[1] Brinton (1901:73, 108-109, 113, 133) in the first general book written on the Indians of the New World adopted the Powell classification.

[2] Latham (1856:77) made the same suggestion earlier, but on what grounds it is not clear.

Kroeber (1925; 1940:463-470), Sturtevant (1959), Heizer (1952; 1955), Davis (1963), Hoijer (1941; 1946:9-29), Swanton (1952:1-10), Goddard (1914), Chamberlain (1910), Bright (1964), Hodge (1907:vi-vii). From these accounts the reader may easily determine what work has been done in the last 40 or 50 years in California.

A wider perspective of American Indian tribes and their territories can be found in Swanton (1952), Kroeber (1939), Trager and Harbin (1958), Driver (1961), Spencer, Jennings, *et al.* (1965), and Murdock (1960).

The reader who wishes to orient himself in the variety and complexity of California Indian cultures will find most useful the three University of California scientific series: 1) *Publications in American Archaeology and Ethnology* (vols. 1-50, 1903-1964); 2) *Anthropological Records* (vols. 1-22, 1937-1965); and, 3) *Publications in Anthropology* (vols. 1-2, 1964-1965). The single best book is, of course, Kroeber's *Handbook of the Indians of California* (1925); also useful is the source book, *The California Indians,* edited by Heizer and Whipple (1951).

MAPS OF CALIFORNIA TRIBES PUBLISHED BEFORE 1925

The Spanish and Mexicans who held California until 1850 did not make maps on which tribal groups were located. In 1844, Duflot de Mofras, a French explorer, drew up and published a map which showed the general location of a number of California tribes according to the then-current ideas of their placements. It is relatively accurate, though no boundary lines are shown.

The first map drawn up with the aim of showing the location of all known tribes was prepared by Alexander S. Taylor in 1864. This map came into the possession of the historian, Hubert H. Bancroft, who refers to it in his *Native Races,* but it was not until 1941 that the map was published with lists and an attempted identification of the names (Heizer, 1941). As might be expected, the names appearing on Taylor's map are rather variable as regards spelling, and not all are tribal entities, some of them being village names or tribelet names, and some are unidentifiable. In the light of how little systematic ethnographic work had been done in California by 1864, the map is remarkable for its completeness and accuracy.

Stephen Powers (1877) published the first map which showed tribal boundaries. Map 2 of the present paper shows these boundaries as determined by Powers. From what Powers wrote, it can be assumed that the tribal areas were determined from information which he himself elicited from informants while doing field work between 1872 and 1875.

In 1891 Powell published a map, entitled "Linguistic Families of American Indians North of Mexico," which indicated the boundaries of the stocks or families in California. This map was subsequently reissued apparently several times, with corrections based upon newer information. We have reproduced here (Map 3) the revised boundaries as shown on the version of the Powell map issued in 1910 as an accompaniment to the *Handbook of American Indians North of Mexico,* edited by F. W. Hodge (1910).

THE REVISED KROEBER MAP OF 1925

The Kroeber map, published in 1925 in the *Handbook of the Indians of California,* was completed in 1918 and was based upon published information (of which there was a considerable quantity if one judges from the bibliography cited by Kroeber, 1925:943-966) and unpublished information collected by Kroeber or by ethnologists working for or in cooperation with the University of California. The 1925 map could not have been prepared much before March, 1918, because at that time Dixon and Kroeber sent to the Editorial Committee of the University of California their monograph, *Linguistic Families of California,* which was published in September, 1919, and which contained the information supporting the reduction of California language families to seven. The only major change which has since been made in the direction of further stock reduction is that Lutuamian (represented in California only by the Modoc) was classed by Sapir as a Penutian language.[3]

In 1955 Kroeber and I, in connection with our services on behalf of the Indians of California who were plaintiffs in a suit against the United States,[4] went over the 1925 map of California tribes and made certain changes on the basis of information acquired in the intervening years. These changes are not very great, but they are worth mentioning. The narrow peninsula of Washo

[3] Hoijer (1946:15) notes that Lutuamian (represented in California by the Modoc) is classified by M. Jacobs (1930) as Sahaptin.

[4] For Kroeber's part in this, see Stewart, 1961.

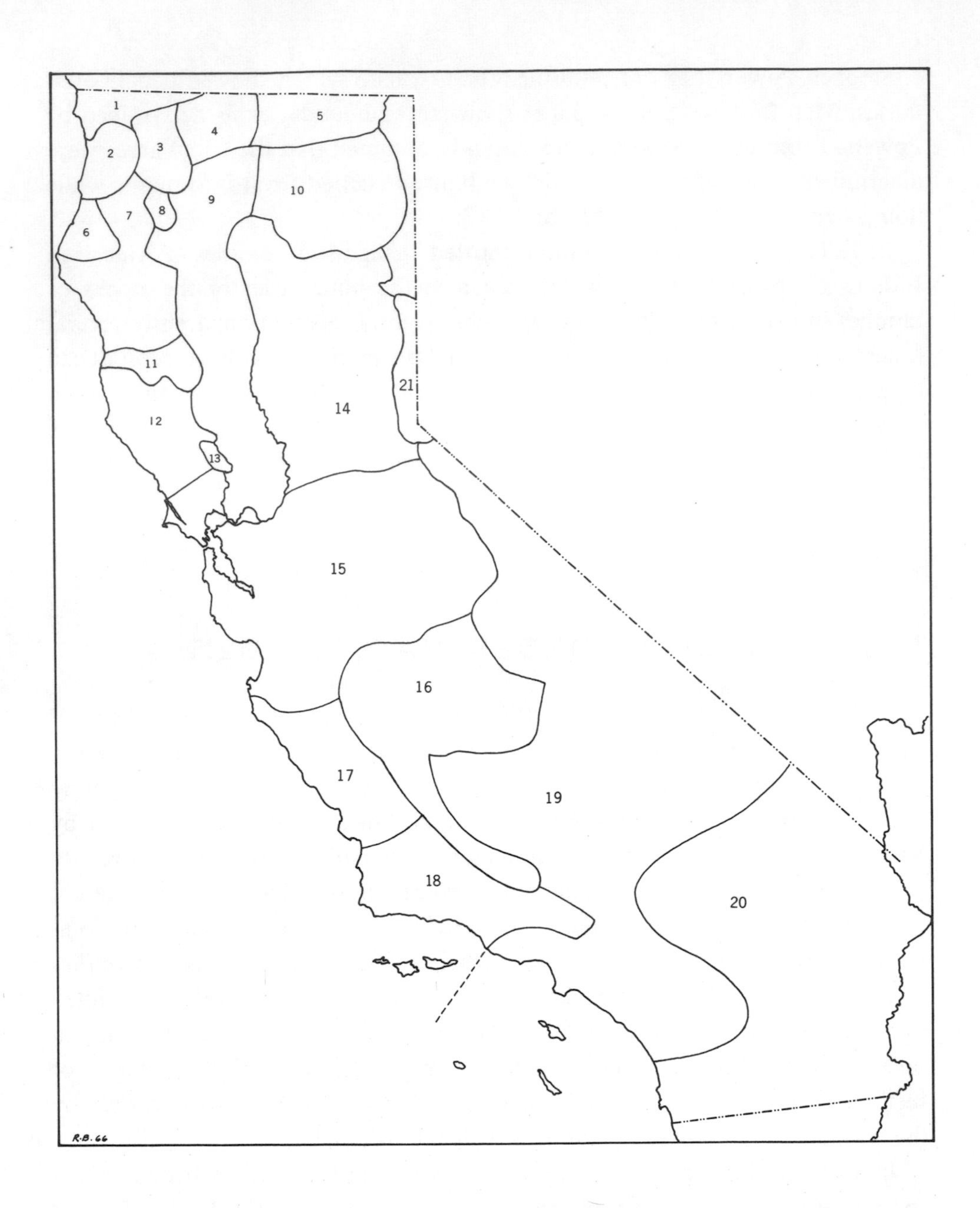

MAP 2. LANGUAGE-TRIBAL GROUPS OF POWERS, 1877. 1. Tinneh [Tolowa]. 2. Yurok. 3. Karok. 4. Shasta. 5. Modok. 6. Wishosk. 7. Tinneh [Hupa, *et al.*]. 8. Chimariko. 9. Wintun. 10. Achomawi. 11. Yuki [Coast, Interior]. 12. Pomo. 13. Yuki [Wappo]. 14. Maidu. 15. Mutsun. 16. Yokuts. 17. San Antonio. 18. Santa Barbara. 19. Shoshoni. 20. Yuma. 21. Washo.

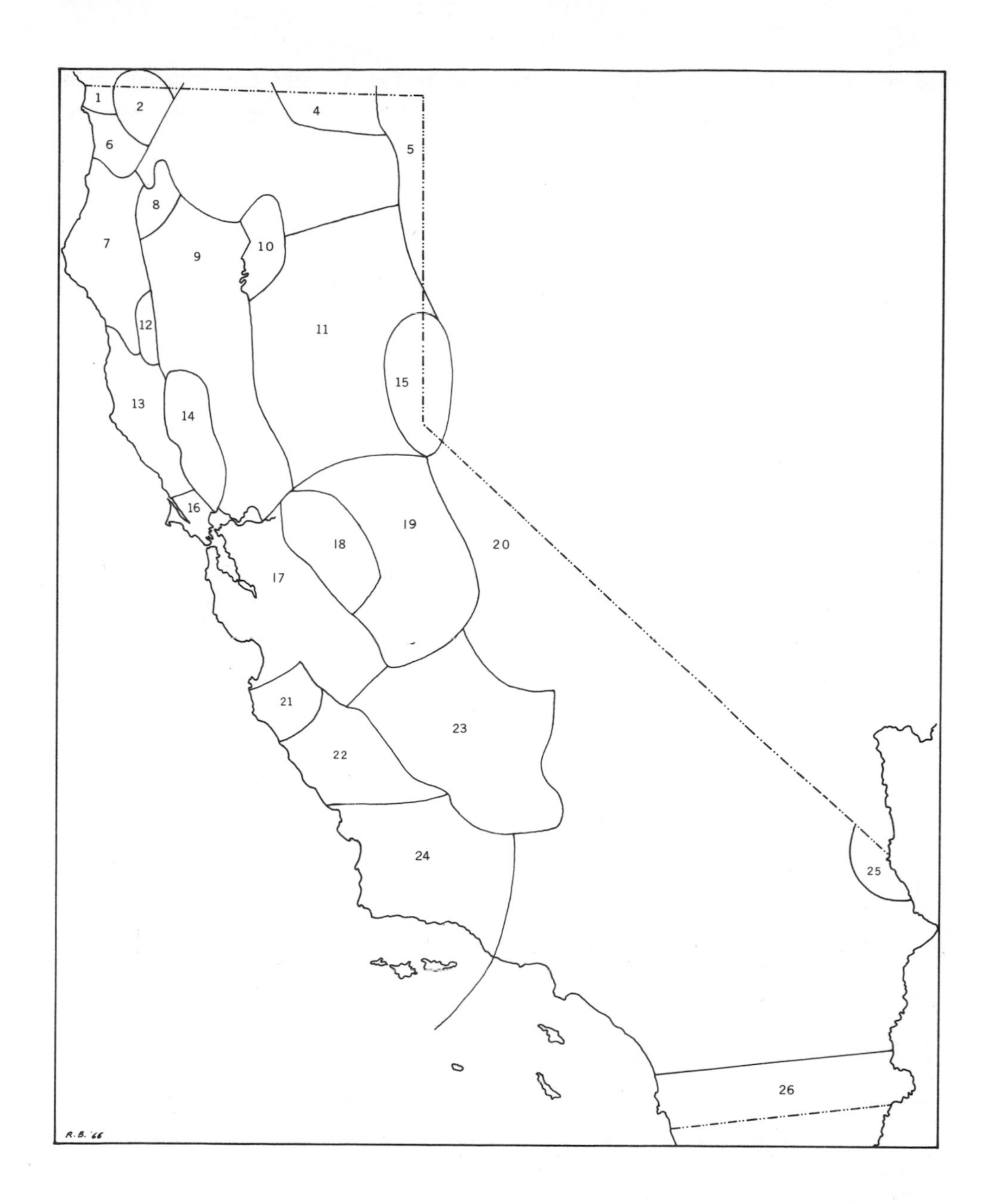

MAP 3. LANGUAGE STOCKS OF POWELL, 1891. 1. Athapascan [Tolowa]. 2. Quoratean [Karok]. 3. Shastan. 4. Lutuami. 5. Shoshonean. 6. Weitspekan. 7. Athapascan [Hupa, *et al.*]. 8. Chimarikan. 9. Copehan [Wintun]. 10. Yanan. 11. Pujunan [Maidu]. 12. Yukian. 13. Kulanapan [Pomo]. 14. Yukian [Wappo]. 15. Washoan. 16. Moquelumnan [Coast Miwok]. 17. Costanoan. 18. Mariposan [Yokuts]. 19. Moquelumnan [Sierra Miwok]. 20. Shoshonean. 21. Esselenian. 22. Salinan. 23. Mariposan [Yokuts]. 24. Chumashan. 25. Yuman [Mohave]. 26. Yuman [Diegueño, Yuma].

territory extending southwesterly has been retracted, and the area has been assigned equally to the Southern Maidu (Nisenan) and Northern Sierra Miwok. The western limits of Washo territory, falling along the crest of the Sierra Nevadas, is not only more likely, but further it is known that the little southwestern extension appearing on the 1925 map was due to misinterpretation of information from Washo informants who said that on occasion they hunted in the area; evidence for more than transient forays into this strip is lacking. The tribal territory earlier assigned to the "Eastern Mono" (Kroeber, 1925:586) has been divided into two areas, both of which are renamed as Mono Lake Paiute and Owens Valley Paiute, which were differentiated by Steward (1933:235-237; see also Kroeber 1959:264-269). In default of precise information on territorial boundaries, Kroeber estimated these in the 1925 map by drawing straight lines for several of the Shoshonean tribes of the desert interior of Southern California. The "Koso," named and mapped by Kroeber (1925:589), are the Shoshoni of the Koso Mountains, Panamint Valley, and Death Valley, and are now called Panamint Shoshoni (Steward, 1937:626; 1938:76). While some uncertainties still, and perhaps always will, exist as to actual territorial boundaries, work done since the 1930's allows much more accurate lines to be drawn for the desert area of California.

The Saclan (or Saklan) group, which was classed as doubtfully Costanoan by Kroeber in 1925, has now proved, after analysis of the vocabulary in Arroyo de la Cuesta's *Idiomas Californias* by M. Beeler (1955), to be a Miwok language most closely affiliated with the two northern Sierra dialects of eastern Miwok (see also Beeler, 1959; Kroeber, 1959:272).[5] The presence

[5] A copy of the *Idiomas* has been since 1878 in the Bureau of American Ethnology files. It was copied in that year by E. F. Murray of Philadelphia from the original manuscript, then at Santa Barbara Mission. A. S. Gatschet studied, but did not publish, the *Idiomas* data and wrote the following comment on the copy at the end of the Saclan vocabulary: "Is Mutsun and stands between Chokoyem [i.e., Coast Miwok] and Tuolumne [i.e., Central Sierra Miwok]." C. Hart Merriam made a copy of the Bureau of American Ethnology *Idiomas* in 1916, and then corrected his copy in 1919 by comparing it with the original manuscript, which was by that time in the Bancroft Library. Merriam wrote on his copy of the Saclan vocabulary, "Compared by me with my Mokozumne, Wipa and other Mewko dialects and found to be essentially the same." It thus appears that Kroeber, who once cited (1904:50) the *Idiomas,* did not have access to Arroyo's Saclan data or he would not have classified it as "doubtfully Costanoan." Kroeber (1910) did not cite or use the word lists in Arroyo's *Idiomas* when he analyzed the Chumash and Costanoan languages, yet in the same year in the *Handbook of American Indians* (Hodge, 1910:402) Saclan is identified in an unsigned article as Costanoan and Arroyo's *Idiomas* manuscript is cited. Kroeber does say (1925:463) that Saclan "may be suspected of having shown particular affinities to Wintun, Miwok, or Yokuts." Beeler (1955) was, therefore, the first to publish the identification of Saclan, although this identification was known earlier by Gatschet and Merriam. Arroyo himself (see below) recognized that Saclan was "entirely different" from Juchiun and Karkin (Costanoan).

of a Miwok group living on the south shore of Carquinez Straits immediately raises the question of whether there was, in aboriginal times, a relatively continuous band of Miwok groups extending from the Coast Miwok through the Saclan of the south shore of Suisun Bay and across the delta to join with the Sierra Miwok. This question is not a new one; it was first raised by Merriam (1907), shortly afterward discussed by Barrett (1908) and Kroeber (1908*a*), and subsequently commented upon (in an unsigned prefatory comment) by myself in Merriam (1955:133-134), by Beeler (1955, 1959), by Callaghan (1964:46), and by Kroeber (1957:215-217; 1959:269-277). The problem is an important one with regard to a map showing tribal distribution, since one is either inclined to accept a Bay Miwok group joining a Plains Miwok group, which in turn shares a common boundary with Northern Sierra Miwok (as shown by Callaghan, 1964: map opp. 49; and as suggested by the map in Merriam [1907] with the addition of the Saclan or Bay Miwok), or he takes the more conservative view of "not proven" and accepts the Delta region as occupied by Northern Valley Yokuts, which is the position taken by Kroeber. We adopt the Merriam-Beeler-Callaghan suggestion and have so indicated it on the revised 1925 Kroeber map (Map 4). Schenck (1926) and Cook (1957) have reviewed the Spanish documents and have drawn up maps showing the location of named aboriginal groups living along the East Bay shore of Alameda and Contra Costa counties and the Sacramento-San Joaquin delta area.[6] Cook (1957:142) concludes that the Saclan group probably lived in the Lafayette-Walnut Creek area, and this is consistent with other evidence which indicates that the village by the name of Saclan (perhaps the tribelet center) lay just north of Lafayette on a feeder of Reliez Creek. The Coast Miwok have been assigned ownership of the Sonoma Valley as proposed by Kroeber (1957:216), this boundary shift being at the expense of territory formerly mapped as Patwin. With the assignment of the Saclan as Bay Miwok, we now have a Costanoan-speaking area, about which very little is known, in Alameda County bounded on the west by San Francisco Bay, on the north by San Pablo Bay, on the east by Walnut Creek, and on the south by a line running east and west between Oakland and San Leandro. In the north are two identifiable groups, the Karkin and Juichun (Cook, 1957, renders the latter group as Huchiun). Both the Karkin and Juichun languages are represented by vocabularies in Arroyo's *Idiomas*. Arroyo himself wrote at the end of the Saclan vocabulary, "Here [at the mission in San Francisco, January 17,

[6] The most important and detailed study to date of the Plains Miwok is by J. A. Bennyhoff (n.d.) in his doctoral dissertation. This is not published, but a copy is available for reference in the Art-Anthropology Library, University of California (Berkeley).

1821] I saw the Saclan, which pleased me very much, and it is postpositive, as I said at the beginning. Karkin and Juichun is one language, the Saclan is another entirely different." The Bureau of American Ethnology copy of Arroyo's *Idiomas* bears the following notation by Gatschet at the end of the Juichun vocabulary: "Closely related to the Mutsun of San Juan Bautista." Merriam has written at the top of his copy of the Juichun vocabulary, "According to my vocabularies, Juichun comes nearest to the Olhonean (i.e., Costanoan) of Santa Clara. It is not very close to Hoo-mon-twash ['Mutsun']. CHM." Arroyo himself had an opinion on the matter, and he wrote at the end of the Juichun vocabulary, "Finally these words resemble more clearly the Mutsun of San Juan Bautista than those of the Karkin, all of them having been the same in origin." This remark is consistent with that made by him, and quoted above, in connection with the affinities of Karkin. There are several comments on the Karkin vocabulary of Arroyo. Gatschet wrote, "Is clearly Mutsun but differs largely from all vocabularies in contributions. It comes nearest Sa. Clara dialect." Merriam, on his copy, wrote, "Comparison with my Olhonean vocabularies show Karkin to be unmistakably Olhonean, and nearest to 'Santa Clara' of my meagre series." Arroyo wrote, "Wondering I waited to hear numbers as in Mutsun of San Juan Bautista, and said: 'This is the origin of the language of San Francisco, San Jose, Santa Clara, Santa Cruz, San Juan Bautista, San Carlos, and Soledad, as far as the Chalones of this last, but so varied in each mission that in each it appears to be a distinct language, and it is not in reality like what anyone may see and observe. This language extends for 45 to 50 leagues from N. to S. The *Karkin,* which signifies to barter, are also called Sutsunu.' " There is, thus, general agreement on the fact that both Juichun and Karkin are Costanoan. Beeler's and Merriam's analysis indicates that Juichun is related to the Santa Clara dialect, which extends to the south as far as San Jose. I have taken the liberty, therefore, of naming the divergent Karkin dialect "San Pablo Costanoan" in an effort to retain a Spanish name of the general type assigned to several of the Costanoan dialects. Arroyo's statement that the Karkin are also called Sutsunu (i.e., Suisun) is apparently incorrect, there being evidence (cf. Kroeber, 1932: 352-355) that the Suisun are southern Patwin. Since the Karkin apparently held the north shore of Carquinez Straits (Kroeber, 1957:217), the territory of the San Pablo Costanoan dialect has been extended to include this stretch. Broadbent (1957) includes in her discussion of Rumsen Costanoan a useful summary of the dialect divisions of this language.

A reclassification of the Athabascan tribes of Northwestern California by Baumhoff (1958) has been accepted as providing better evidence of tribal identities and territories than that of Kroeber (1925). Major changes proposed by Baumhoff are: deletion of the Chilula who are nothing more than the Whilkut of lower Redwood Creek (pp. 202-203); establishment of two Sinkyone groups (Map 2); and acceptance of Nomland's (1938) Bear River group.

Our listing here of those ethnic groups whose names and locations have been determined and mapped by Kroeber and Merriam is, no doubt, somewhat incomplete. Almost certainly some small groups which were territorially and politically, as well as linguistically, separate became extinct before a clear record of their existence was made. By way of example, the Giamina, a small Shoshonean speaking tribe on Poso Creek, are suspected of having existed in fact, but we cannot be wholly certain that this was the case. Kroeber (1907: 126-127) gives us what details we possess about the Giamina, who may be the same group as an equally little-known hill tribe called the Kumachisi. Let us note another instance. The language spoken on San Nicolas Island is known to us primarily from four words which are said to have been learned by George Nidever from an old Nicoleño woman whom he rescued from the island in 1836, after she had lived there alone for 18 years. The available records of this unusual marooning have been published (Heizer and Elsasser, 1963), and the four words mentioned were first published by Hardacre (1880), and shortly afterward by Thompson and West (1883) in slightly different form. They are:

	Hardacre	Thompson and West
Hide (skin)	to–co (to–kay′)	tocah
Man	nache (nah′–chey)	nache
Sky	te–gua (tay′–gwah)	toygwah
Body	pinche (pin–oo–chey)	puoo–chay

Probably some printer's errors are involved here in accounting for differences between the two lists. Thus, one might guess that Hardacre's *pinche* should read *pinuche,* and that Thompson and West's *puoo–chey* should read *pinoo–chey*. Since the time when this single variant list of four words was commented on by Kroeber (1907:153) with the opinion that the vocabulary was Shoshonean, very little additional information has come to light. A. Pinart in 1878 (in Heizer, 1952:50, 72) recorded that the Indians of San Nicolas Island were called *xax'asat* in the Chumash language of Santa Cruz Island, and that the Nicoleño were called *Niminokots* in the language of the Ventura Chumash. What seems clear from the accounts written by the persons who made the dramatic rescue of the woman in or about the year 1836 (see Heizer and Elsasser, 1963:135, 140-141, 145) is that she did not speak a Chumash language, but we cannot be certain that Hardacre was correct in saying, nearly 40 years after the event, that the priest at Santa Barbara brought an Indian from San Fernando (i.e., a speaker of the Fernandeño dialect of Shoshonean Gabrielino) to see the woman and that he could not understand her speech. The difficulties of resolving the question of whether the probably Shoshonean dialect of San Nicolas Island was closer to Gabrielino or Luiseño, geographically the nearest Shoshonean languages, or (by reason of its insular remoteness) whether it was perhaps sufficiently differentiated from the mainland Shoshonean dialects to constitute a truly distinctive and separate language are so great that the question may never be settled with the little information we now possess.

Another kind of complicated unravelling of confusing and tangled ethnographic testimony concerns the territorial placement of the several tribes along that stretch of the Colorado River which now forms the joint boundary of the states of California and Arizona. Between the time of Alarcon and Melchior Diaz in 1540, Onate in 1605, Kino in 1702, Anza in 1775, and Father Garces in 1776 (when he visited the Colorado River people and wrote his diaries and recorded the names and locations of the groups he saw), and the first half of the twentieth century when Kroeber and Spier made ethnological investigations among the River tribes, a good many substantial shifts in habitat occurred. These are discussed by Spier (1933:Chap. 1) and Kroeber (1920; 1925: 799-803), and the Kroeber map reproduced here (Map 4) shows the location of the Colorado River groups as they were about 1830.

These are the kinds of questions which continually make their appearance when one must try to reach conclusions on a large subject where data of uneven value are available. But they are the same questions that scholars in the future will return to and attempt to settle, for, until they are either solved or determined as being insoluble, we shall not know as much as we want to know about the California Indians.

THE C. HART MERRIAM TRIBAL MAP

Dr. Merriam spent over 30 years of his life engaged in the study of California Indians (Kroeber, 1955*a*). Trained as a biologist, he was interested in the geographical distribution of animal species. When his chief interest shifted to

Indians, his approach, wrote Kroeber (1955*a*:viii-ix), "merely swung from questions of the precise ranges occupied by species and subspecies to the problems of the exact location of aboriginal human languages, tribes, villages, beliefs, and customs." The result of investigation based upon this kind of approach yielded information which is characterized both by abundance and detail. Definitely secondary to Merriam's interests was the kind of data which professionally trained anthropologists were securing from 1900 on in California. Merriam did publish some papers on Indian basketry, totemism, mythology, and economy (see Merriam, 1955, especially pp. 228-229), but most of what he wrote on California Indians deals with the identification, classification, and distribution of native groups. Much more information was in his possession, in either record or manuscript form, than he ever published. He was a perfectionist, and had he lived long enough he might have ultimately drawn up and published a map showing the distribution of linguistic families, dialect groups, and tribelets. Over the years of his work, he drew on hundreds of maps of all kinds (USGS quadrangle sheets, oil company road maps, and other maps of the state of California) the areas occupied by tribes which he had investigated. These have all been consulted in connection with the present work.

The basis of both the Kroeber and Merriam maps is the same – linguistic. Both Kroeber and Merriam worked independently, though each could read what the other wrote. Merriam was not a trained linguist in any sense (see Kroeber, 1955*a*:ix-xii), but he worked at comparing vocabularies, which he himself collected from living informants or copied from manuscript or published sources, in much the same way that Powell and his aides had done in the preparation of the 1891 classification of North American linguistic stocks. Two languages which he could see as clearly related when he matched the two vocabularies, or linguistic relationships which he accepted as demonstrated by the work of others such as Gatschet, Powell, Powers, or Kroeber, he called a stock. This very simple method for detecting two languages which are related will, however, not take one very far into genetic classification. The result was, therefore, that whereas Dixon and Kroeber (1919) established seven linguistic stocks or families of California Indian languages, Merriam recognized 25. The following table not only introduces the reader to Merriam's terminology, but also provides a synonymy of the linguistic stock names established by Powers, Powell, Dixon, and Kroeber. The Powers classification of 1877 is given to make possible a comparison with the Merriam and Kroeber names. I do not know to what extent Powell, author of the appendix to Powers' 1877 book, followed the lead of Powers, or to what extent Powers took his cue from Powell.[7] Powers' map (Map 2) shows the territories of the 19 stocks listed in the following table, but Powell in the appendix of Powers' volume identifies only 13 families with certainty (14 if we include the San Antonio Mission language as a separate family). The stocks mentioned by Powers, but not Powell, are the Tinneh (i.e., Athabascan), Modoc (formerly Lutuamian but today classed as Penutian), Yuma (i.e., Hokan), Washo (Hokan), Wintun (Penutian), and Shoshoni (Shoshonean). Powell was, we may be certain, not unaware of the existence of all of these languages (see Map 3), but he did not analyze vocabularies of these speech forms in the 1877 work. If we were to make a guess based upon his map (Map 3) and classification of 1891, it would be that he would have agreed with Powers on the reality of the Tinneh or Athapascan, Modoc or Lutuamian, Yuma or Yuman, Washo or Washoan, Wintun or Copehan, and Shoshoni or Shoshonean as families. What we see in this simple comparison is that the Powell classification of California languages was, in 1877, already pretty well solidified into the form in which he was to present it in 1891 as part of the larger picture of North American Indian language stocks.

It is not claimed that the two maps of tribal distributions, one by Merriam (Map 5) and the other by Kroeber (Map 4), presented here are free from error, but they do represent a considerable improvement on any maps now available. The maps will help those persons who wish to know what group occupied a particular territory; they will be of aid in future demographic studies of the type that Baumhoff (1958) and Cook (1955, 1956, 1957) have already begun; and they will be of use to archaeologists in their efforts to determine the identity and distribution of late prehistoric and historic types of tribal culture. As linguists proceed with their work of determining the precise degree of relationships between languages of single stocks and propose, through lexicostatistic dating, the periods of time which have elapsed since two languages separated from each other, archaeologists will try to find evidence for replacements of population in prehistoric occupation sites. Not much has yet been done along this line, the work of Baumhoff and Olmsted (1964) being the main example for California, but it can be anticipated that much more such inquiry will be made in the future. When this is done, reliable maps of tribal territories will be a necessary aid.

[7] Neither Powell nor Powers were trained linguists, but both had a great deal of common sense. Powers (1877:197, 45) gives comparative word lists of Yuki, Huchnom, and Wappo which show these three to be related, and a comparative list of Yurok, Karok, and Modoc to illustrate the linguistic separateness of the Klamath River tribes.

LINGUISTIC STOCKS OR FAMILIES AS NAMED AND MAPPED BY MERRIAM, KROEBER (1925), POWERS (1877), AND POWELL (1891)[a]

Merriam	Kroeber	Powers[b]	Powell
Athapaskan	Athabascan	Tinneh	Athapascan
Yukean	Yukian	Yu–ki	Yukian
Lutuamean	Lutuamian	Mo–dok	Lutuamian
Shastan	Hokan	Shas–ta	Shastan[c]
Achomawan		A–cho–ma–wi	....
Kahrok		Ka–rok	Quoratean
Tlohomtahoi		....	....
Chimareko		Chim–a–ri–ko	Chimarikan[d]
Yahnah		....	Yanan
Pomoan		Po–mo	Kulanapan
Chumash		Santa Barbara	Chumashan
Yuman		Yuma	Yuman
Washoo		Washo	Washoan
Esselen		....	Esselenian
Ennesen		....	Salinan
Olhonean	Penutian	Mut–sun	Costanoan
Wintoon		Win–tun	Copehan
Midoo		Mai–du	Pujunan
Mewan		....	Moquelumnan
Yokut		Yo–kuts	Mariposan
Shoshonean	Shoshonean	Sho–sho–ni	Shoshonean
Tongva		....	....
Tubotelobela		....	....
Polikla	Algonkian	Yurok	Weitspekan
Soolahteluk		Wishosk	Wishoskan[e]

[a] See Bonnerjea (1963: 723-724) for list of later editions (1906, 1915, 1926) of the Powell map of 1891.

[b] Powers did not make investigations south of San Francisco on the coast, or south of Tehachapi in the interior, or east of the Sierras in eastern California.

[c] Spelled "Sastean" in Powell's text.

[d] Listed in Powell's text (p. 63), but name omitted from map.

[e] Misspelled on map (Wishokan).

THE NATURE OF TRIBAL TERRITORIES AND BOUNDARY LINES IN CALIFORNIA

All of the maps which have been prepared (e.g., Powers, 1877; Kroeber, 1925; Merriam, MSS), as well as published maps in monographic treatments of individual tribes such as those in the *University of California Publications in American Archaeology and Ethnology* or the *University of California Anthropological Records,* are based upon information provided by the firsthand testimony of California natives. While attempts have been made to throw doubts upon the reality of land ownership by Indians (see Wheeler-Voegelin, 1956), it nevertheless seems clear that definite land-ownership concepts existed among most, if not all, California Indians. The idea that a certain, definable extent of territory was owned and that the plants, animals, minerals, and the like attached to that land were also owned by the claimants is supported by an abundance of statements made by Indians to that effect.[8] Since the question exists, it seems worthwhile here to refer to some of the recorded documentation which supports the concept of exclusive land ownership and precise territorial boundaries.

Actual boundary markers, either artificial in the form of wooden posts or stone cairns, or natural in the form of streams or lakes, are reported for the Yokuts (Stewart, 1927:390) and Yuki (Powers, 1877:109). The most common boundary markers for tribal lands were drainage systems marked by watersheds (Kroeber, 1925:160-161), so that borders were often marked by mountain peaks or ridges or long summits (cf. DuBois, 1935:4; de Angulo and Freeland, 1929:314-316; Nomland, 1938:91; Stewart, 1943:32-33; Drucker, 1937:29; Thompson, 1916:27; Powers, 1877:66; Barrett, 1908:232; Gifford, 1939:296-297, 301, and 1923:81, 85; Waterman, 1920:221; Goddard, 1923:101, 104). At times, and probably much more commonly than has been reported in the ethnographical literature, a prominent rock outcrop (cf. Spott and Kroeber, 1942:182; Powers, 1877:66, 109) or certain special trees (Loud, 1918:252-253) were recognized as marking the border between two groups. The Pomo are reported by Stewart (1943:32-33) and Loeb (1926:197) to teach their children the boundary markers so they will not stray beyond their own territory and be shot for trespassing.

For ourselves, participants of mid-twentieth century culture with rapid

[8] See Heizer (1958) for a discussion of aboriginal maps, usually recorded by early explorers, on which were indicated terrain features.

transport and worldwide verbal communication only as far distant as the nearest telephone, it is difficult to appreciate a world populated, as was the New World in 1492, by thousands of small, close-knit ethnic groups ("tribes," "bands," "tribelets," and the like) who had no realistic conception of the immensity of the earth, and whose members might spend their whole lives in the space of 100 square miles. What variety life offered depended upon what the village provided, or, in exceptional cases, upon the chance to see beyond the familiar terrain the lands of another, closely neighboring group which might be visited on a trading expedition, or a rare trip to view or participate in a great ceremonial rite. Seasonal movement of valley groups to the cooler mountain areas offered a pleasant interlude in what might otherwise be a wholly routine existence. By and large, each of the 500 or so tribelets of aboriginal California comprised essentially separate wholes or as Redfield (1955) termed them, "ecological systems." It would be incorrect to unduly stress the degree to which each was isolated, for there were contacts with neighbors and communication across all borders. Most of these contacts were of a peaceful nature, but even warfare was a form of contact between two groups. A more meaningful way to describe the circumscribed outlook of most California Indian groups is to say that they were socially and economically self-sufficient.

A few quotations from Kroeber's *Handbook* (1925) will illustrate the particularities of the Weltanschauung of California Indians. About the Yurok of the Klamath River, Kroeber (1925:13) wrote:

The national horizon of the Yurok was as confined as that of most northern Californians. Adjacent tribes [i.e., Tolowa, Hupa, Karok and Wiyot] were visited at ceremonies and to some extent wives were purchased from them. Of those next beyond, there was only the dimmest knowledge; and farther, neither rumor nor legend nor interest. At that distance, there was only the end of the world, or a strange unsighted ocean, and perhaps things that no one wanted to see. The Yurok did not venture into the unknown and felt no desire to. Nor did they welcome strangers. If any came, it must be for a bad purpose; and they were put out of the way at the first opportunity. A man of substance, wealth, or character did not stray or nose about. He remained at home in dignity, or traveled where relatives of old or hereditary friends welcomed him. If ever he went farther, it was with their introduction.

Of the Sinkyone whose territory lay on the South Fork of Eel River, Kroeber (1925:145) wrote:

The narrow horizon of many of the Californian tribes is illustrated by the travels of an old Sinkyone, who was born and lived and died at the mouth of Bull Creek. He recited that in the course of his years he had been downstream to the Wiyot boundary, upstream to one of the South Fork tributaries still in Sinkyone territory, coastward to the Mattole River, and inland to the ridge beyond which lies the Van Dusen Fork. A circle with a 20-mile radius around Dyerville would more than include this little world of his life's experience.

Of the Maidu of the northern Sierras, Kroeber (1925:395) has nearly the same to say:

Twenty miles is said to have been an unusual distance for a hill or mountain Maidu to travel. In the valley journeys may have been longer. No northern Californian would go far from his home. Beyond a dozen or two villages there lay a narrow belt known only by hearsay or through occasional meetings with other visitors. Everything farther was utterly unknown. It is probable that the westermost Maidu had only the vaguest cognizance, if any, of the most easterly Pomo; and the intervening Wintun occupied a comparatively narrow and open strip of land. Even within a man's ken, half the villages were likely to be hostile or under suspicion.

An interesting and instructive example of the provincialism of aboriginal California natives is provided by information secured by E. W. Gifford about 1915 from a Northfork Mono Indian woman named Wiunu who claimed at that time to be 95 years of age, and who was, therefore, born about 1820. At the age of seven or eight she had been taken across the Sierra Nevadas to Mono County where she spent the winter, but except for this one excursion she lived all her life in her own tribal territory. In the course of time she married, and during her life she established successive residences in no fewer than 23 separate villages within the group's territory which is in Madera County, just north of the San Joaquin River, a few miles northwest of Shaver Lake. In her early years she lived with her mother after her father's death, and after her mother's death she lived with her half-sister. After her marriage she again made several moves, the reasons for these translocations being either because of her husband's death, because of interference with native life by the whites, or occasionally "just to be moving." Since the location of each village is mapped, all of this changing of places of residence occurred within an area which can be computed as not exceeding 67 square miles or as a rectangle 9 by 7½ miles on the sides. We do not know how typical such an individual's experience may have been, but in general the data available suggest that it was not at all unusual for a person to spend his entire lifetime within such a limited range of territory.

Of the Miwok of the central Sierras, Kroeber (1925:444) writes in a similar vein:

Among themselves the Miwok are content to refer to one another by village, or employ an endless succession of "northerners" and similar directional names that never crystallize into specific designations. The same people that are northerners to their neighbors on one side are southerners to those on the other, and so on ad infinitum, even beyond the boundaries of the stock, as far as knowledge extends. A group of people as a unit possessing an existence and therefore a name of its own is a concept that has not dawned on the Miwok. Humanity must appear to them like a uniform sheet spread over an endless earth, differentiable only with reference to one's own location in the whole. A national sense is weak enough among most of the California Indians; but there are usually a few generic names for outside groups of foreigners. If the Miwok have such, they have not become known; except Koyuwe-k, "salt people," for the Mono. Even the Washo are only "easterners" or "uplanders." Lisnayu-k denotes either the Yokuts or the Costanoans of the vicinity of Pacheco Pass. Their four standard terms are Tamuleko, Tamulek, or Tumitok, northerners; Chumetoko, Chumetok, or Chumteya, southerners; Hisotoko, Hisatok, or Hittoya, easterners; Olowitoko, Olowitok, Olokok, or Olwiya, westerners; or other close dialectic variants.

There is a great deal of information in ethnographic accounts concerning the defense of territory against trespassers. Since the advantage of owning land for exclusive use lay in the fact that the owners could count on the animal and plant food it produced for their economic support, it is not surprising to learn that when trespassers were found it was assumed, and generally with good reason, that they were present to steal food that did not belong to them. The reaction of the land-owning group was to try to kill poachers, since they were almost literally taking the food out of the owners' mouths. Indeed, boundary trespass turns out to be the major cause of intergroup fighting, or warfare if these skirmishes could be so termed. By way of example, we cite instances of fighting resulting from trespass for the following groups: Southern Maidu (Beals, 1933:362, 364, 366; Voegelin, 1942:179); Atsugewi (Garth, 1953: 185); Yana (Gifford and Klimek, 1936:85, 95); Achomawi (Voegelin, 1942:180, 209; Sapir and Spier, 1941:269); Wintu (DuBois, 1935:18); Northern Maidu (Dixon, 1905:201-225); Yokuts and Owens Valley Paiute (Driver, 1937:94); Western Mono, Yokuts, and Miwok (Aginsky, 1943:434, elements 1709, 109*a*); Pomo, Lassik, Kato, and Yuki (Essene, 1942:39, element 1727); Pomo (Stewart, 1943:38, 43, 45; Loeb, 1926:197, 200, 210; Barrett, 1952:50, 192; Gifford and Kroeber, 1937:121, 122, 155); tribes of northwestern California (Driver, 1939:358); Southern Diegueño (Gifford, 1918:173; Spier, 1923:306); Desert Cahuilla and Luiseño (Strong, 1929:40, 279; Hooper, 1920:355); Owens Valley Paiute (Stewart, 1937:631); Surprise Valley Paiute (Kelley, 1932:185); Tolowa (Powers, 1877:66); Yuma (Forde, 191:114-115); Wappo (Driver, 1936:211, 213); Hupa (Curtis, 1924; vol. 13:14; Wallace, 1949:2); Coast Yuki (Gifford, 1939:317); Patwin and Wintun (Kroeber, 1932:297-298, 300-303, 356, 420); Yuki (Foster, 1944:188, 190, 228, 229); Kato (Curtis, 1924; vol. 14:185). The Spanish explorers in the eighteenth century understood the fact of exclusively owned tribal territories as evidence by Longinos' (1938:50) statement that, among the Chumash, wars originate over "rights of boundaries or the places where they gather seeds," and by Fages' (1937:12, 64) statement that wars arise among the Chumash over "disputes concerning fruits of the earth and women" and that the Indians of the Sierra de Santa Lucia (i.e., coastal Salinans) guard and protect acorns and fight trespassers.

A further bit of evidence of ethnographic nature which supports the idea of group territories that were held permanently comes from the common practice of cremating persons dying away from home (while on a shell-gathering expedition to the ocean coast, visiting relatives, on a trading expedition, and the like) and bringing the cremated remains back to his home village. If possible, the body itself was carried home, as in the instance recounted by Bruff in 1850 of a woman who in two and a half days carried her dead husband's corpse from Weitchpec, at the confluence of the Trinity and Klamath Rivers, to Trinidad Bay on the ocean coast (Bruff, 1949:954). The reason usually stated for these practices is that a man wishes to be buried in the same place as his ancestors, and in the place where he was born. It is clear that such a custom is one developed and adhered to by people whose ownership of specific territories was traditional and of long standing. Full documentation from the literature would serve no purpose, but the following references are provided to support this statement. The following tribes practiced this custom: Wailaki (Baumhoff, 1958:176); Kato and Lassik (Essene, 1942:36); Nisenan (Beals, 1933:376); Shasta and Achomawi (Voegelin, 1942:137, 231; Dixon, 1907: 467; Powers 1877:249; Holt, 1946:324); Yana (Gifford and Klimek, 1936: 84, 95; Sapir and Spier, 1941:277); Northern Maidu (Dixon, 1905:246); Coast Yuki (Gifford, 1939:352); Yurok (Heizer and Whipple, 1951:225); Kato, Pomo, and Wailaki (Loeb, 1932:13, 53); Yokuts (Curtis, 1924, vol. 14:160).

LIST OF PUBLISHED DETAILED MAPS SHOWING TRIBAL TERRITORIES

The large maps attached to this report cannot provide the kind of geographical detail that the student interested in the territory of a particular tribe might like to know. It has been thought worthwhile, therefore, to append a list of previously published tribal maps for the sake of ready reference. No claim is made that the list is a complete one, but an effort has been made to include references to maps which show detail. Maps which are known to be inaccurate, based on secondary data, or which are primarily of historical interest, such as those of A. S. Taylor (Heizer, 1941) or Powers (1877), have not been cited.

Athabascan Family

Tolowa. Drucker, 1937: maps 2, 3; Waterman, 1925: Waterman, 1920, map 2.

Hupa. Waterman, 1920: map 2; Merriam, 1930: map opp. p. 292.

Whilkut. Baumhoff. 1958: map 2; Kroeber, 1925: fig. 13; Goddard, 1914: pl. 38.

Mattole. Baumhoff, 1958: map 2.

Nongatl. Baumhoff, 1958: map 2.

Lassik. Baumhoff, 1958: map 2.

Lolangkok Sinkyone. Baumhoff, 1958: map 2; Nomland, 1935: map 1.

Shelter Cove Sinkyone. Baumhoff, 1958: map 2; Nomland, 1935: map 1.

Pitch Wailaki. Baumhoff, 1958: map 2; Goddard, 1923: pl. 2.

North Fork Wailaki. (See Pitch Wailaki.)

Eel River Wailaki. (See Pitch Wailaki.)

Bear River. Nomland, 1938: map 1; Baumhoff, 1958: map 2.

Kato. Baumhoff, 1958: map 2; Barrett, 1908: map 1.

Algonkin Family

Yurok. Kroeber, 1925: fig. 1; Waterman, 1920: map 2.

Wiyot. Loud, 1918: pl. 1; Kroeber, 1925: fig. 10.

Yukian Family

Yuki. Kroeber, 1925: pl. 26; Barrett, 1908: map 1; Foster, 1944: map 1.

Huchnom. (See Yuki.)

Coast Yuki. Gifford, 1939; Kroeber, 1925: pl. 26.
Wappo. Kroeber, 1925: pl. 27.

Hokan Family

Shasta. Dixon, 1907: pl. LIX; Holt, 1946: map 1.
New River Shasta. Merriam, 1930: map opp. p. 292; Dixon, 1907: pl. LIX.
Konomihu. Merriam, 1930: map opp. p. 292.
Okwanuchu. Merriam, 1926: map at front.
Achomawi. Merriam, 1926: map at front; Garth, 1953: map at front.
Atsugewi. Merriam, 1926: map at front; Garth, 1953: map at front.
Yana. Merriam, 1926: map at front; Kroeber, 1925: fig. 30; Waterman, 1918: map 1; Sapir and Spier, 1943: map 1; Dixon, 1905: pl. XXXVIII.
Central Yana. (See Yana.)
Southern Yana. (See Yana.)
Yahi. (See Yana.)
Karok. Merriam, 1930: map opp. p. 292; Dixon, 1907: pl. LIX.
Chimariko: Kroeber, 1925: fig. 8; Merriam, 1930: map opp. p. 292.
Pomo. Barrett, 1908: map 1; Kroeber, 1925: pl. 36; Loeb, 1926: pl. 1; Gifford and Kroeber, 1937: map 1; Kroeber, 1932: map at end; Kniffen, 1939: maps 1, 2, 3.
Washo. Barrett, 1917: map 1; Price, 1962: map 1; Dixon, 1905: pl. XXXVIII; Park, 1938: fig. 1.
Esselen. Kroeber, 1904: map at front.
Salinan. Kroeber, 1904: map at front.
Chumash. Kroeber, 1925: pls. 47, 48.
Northern Diegueño. Drucker, 1937: map at front.
Southern Diegueño. Spier, 1923: fig. A; Drucker, 1937: map at front.
Kamia. Gifford, 1931: pl. 1.
Yuma. Forde, 1931: maps 1, 2.
Halchidhoma. Forde, 1931: maps 1, 2.
Mohave. Kroeber, 1951: maps 1, 2.

Penutian Family

Modoc. Merriam, 1926: map at front.
Northern Wintun. DuBois, 1935: map 1; Kroeber, 1932: map at end.
Central Wintun, (Nomlaki). Goldschmidt, 1951: map following p. 314; Kroeber, 1932: map at end.
Southeastern Wintun. Kroeber, 1932: map at end; Kroeber, 1925: pl. 34.

Southwestern Wintun. Kroeber, 1932: map at end; Kroeber, 1925: pl. 34.

Northwestern Maidu. Dixon, 1905: pl. XXXVIII; Kroeber, 1925: pl. 37.

Northeastern Maidu. Dixon, 1905: pl. XXXVIII; Kroeber, 1925: pl. 37.

Southern Maidu (Nisenan). Dixon, 1905: pl. XXXVIII; Beals, 1933: map 1; Kroeber, 1925: pl. 37.

Coast Miwok. Kroeber, 1925: fig. 32; Kroeber, 1932: map at end; Callaghan, 1964: map opp. p. 49; Barrett, 1908: map 1.

Lake Miwok. Kroeber, 1925: pl. 27; Callaghan, 1964: map opp. p. 49; Kroeber, 1932: map at end; Merriam, 1955: map p. 46 (Tuleyome).

Plains Miwok. Merriam, 1907; Barrett, 1908: map 3; Callaghan, 1964: map opp. p. 49.

Northern Miwok. Merriam, 1907; Barrett, 1908: map 3; Callaghan, 1964: map opp. p. 49; Kroeber, 1925: pl. 37.

Central Miwok. (See Northern Miwok.)

Southern Miwok. (See Northern Miwok.)

San Pablo Costanoan. Callaghan, 1964: map opp. p. 49 (area shown).

San Francisco Costanoan. Kroeber, 1925: fig. 42.

Santa Cruz Costanoan. (See San Francisco Costanoan.)

Santa Clara Costanoan. (See San Francisco Costanoan.)

San Juan Bautista (Mutsun) Costanoan. (See San Francisco Costanoan.)

Monterey Costanoan (Rumsen). (See San Francisco Costanoan.)

Northern Valley Yokuts. Callaghan, 1964: map opp. p. 49; Barrett, 1908: map 3.

Southern Valley Yokuts. Kroeber, 1925: pl. 47; Gayton, 1948, vol. 1: map 1.

Northern Hill Yokuts. Kroeber, 1925: pl. 47.

Kings River Yokuts. Kroeber, 1925: pl. 47; Gayton, 1948, vol. 2: map F.

Tule-Kaweah Yokuts. Kroeber, 1925: pl. 47; Gayton, 1948, vol. 1: map 1.

Poso Creek Yokuts. Kroeber, 1925: pl. 47; Gayton, 1948, vol. 1: map 1.

Buena Vista Yokuts. Kroeber, 1925: pl. 47; Gayton, 1948, vol. 1: map 1.

Uto-Aztekan (Shoshonean) Family

Mono Lake Paiute. Stewart, 1933: map 1; Stewart, 1938: fig. 1.

Owens Valley Paiute. Stewart, 1933: map 2; Stewart, 1938: figs. 1, 7.

Monache (Western Mono). Gayton, 1948: map 1; Kroeber, 1925: pl. 47.

Northern Paiute (Surprise Valley). Kelly, 1932: map 1.

Panamint Shoshoni. Stewart, 1937: fig. 1.

Chemehuevi (Southern Paiute). Kroeber, 1907: map opp. p. 164.

Kawaiisu. Stewart, 1937: fig. 1; Park, 1938: fig. 3.

Tubatulabal. Voegelin, 1938: fig. 1.

Kitanemuk. Kroeber, 1925: pl. 48.

Alliklik. Kroeber, 1925: pl. 48.

Serrano. Benedict, 1924: map opp. p. 366; Strong, 1929: map 1.

Fernandeño. Kroeber, 1925: pls. 48, 57.

Gabrielino. Kroeber, 1907: map opp. p. 164; Kroeber, 1925: pl. 57.

Nicoleño. Kroeber, 1907: map opp. p. 164.

Juaneño. Drucker, 1937: map at front; Kroeber, 1925: pl. 57.

Luiseño. Strong, 1929: map 7; Drucker, 1937: map at front; Kroeber, 1925: pl. 57.

Cupeño. Strong, 1929: maps 5, 6; Drucker, 1937: map at front.

Mountain Cahuilla. Drucker, 1937: map at front.

Desert Cahuilla. Strong, 1929: map 2; Drucker, 1937: map at front.

CLASSIFICATION AND LIST OF CALIFORNIA LINGUISTIC STOCKS AND TRIBES IDENTIFIED BY C. HART MERRIAM

The C. Hart Merriam Collection has been and will continue to be a source of primary ethnological information. Merriam's linguistic stock, tribe, and tribelet names are ones which he assigned himself on the basis of what Indians told him when he inquired into these matters. At certain points Merriam's terminology agrees sufficiently closely with that of Powers, Powell, or Kroeber and his students, so that no difficulty should arise in understanding just what group he is referring to. In other instances, however, Merriam assigned names to groups which have not been used by other investigators. Because Merriam himself published a number of papers on California Indians (cited in Merriam, 1955:227-229), and because there have been since 1950 a number of publications based upon data collected by Merriam in which his group names appear, it is believed that a listing here of the names which he was in the habit of employing will constitute a handy reference for future workers. Variant spellings are given in parentheses to aid in identification where the rendering is sufficiently different to cause a problem of recognition. The Merriam tribal names are cross-referenced in the following table to those published by Kroeber (1925), Powers (1877), and the *Handbook of American Indians* (Hodge, 1907, 1910).

KEY TO KROEBER MAP (MAP 4)

Native Tribes, Groups, Language Families and Dialects of California in 1770

Athabascan Family

Oregon group
- 1a. Rogue River

Tolowa group
- 1b. Tolowa

Hupa group
- 1c. Hupa
- 1d. Whilkut

Mattole group
- 1e. Mattole

Wailaki group
- 1f. Nongatl
- 1g. Lassik
- 1h. Shelter Cove Sinkyone
- 1i. Lolangkok Sinkyone
- 1j. Eel River Wailaki
- 1k. Pitch Wailaki
- 1l. North Fork Wailaki
- 1m. Kato

Bear River group
- 1n. Bear River

Algonkin Family

Yurok
- 2a. Yurok
- 2b. Coast Yurok
- 3. Wiyot

Yukian Family

- 4a. Yuki
- 4b. Huchnom
- 4c. Coast Yuki
- 4d. Wappo

Hokan Family

Shastan
- 6a. Shasta
- 6b. New River Shasta
- 6c. Konomihu
- 6d. Okwanuchu
- 6e. Achomawi (Pit River)
- 6f. Atsugewi (Hat Creek)

Yana
- 7a. Northern Yana
- 7b. Central Yana
- 7c. Southern Yana
- 7d. Yahi
- 8. Karok
- 9. Chimariko

Pomo[9]
- 10a. Northern
- 10b. Central
- 10c. Eastern
- 10d. Southeastern
- 10e. Northeastern
- 10f. Southern
- 10g. Southwestern
- 11. Washo
- 12. Esselen

Salinan
- 13a. Antoniano
- 13b. Migueleño
- 13c. Playano (doubtful)

Chumash
- 14a. Obispeño
- 14b. Purisimeño
- 14c. Ynezeño
- 14d. Barbareño
- 14e. Ventureño
- 14f. Emigdiano
- 14g. Cuyama
- 14h. Island

Yuman
- 15a. Northern (Western) Diegueño

[9] Due to the large number of Pomo groups, a larger scale map showing the Pomo area is provided in the detailed inset on Map 5.

15b. Mountain Diegueño
15c. Southern (Eastern or Desert) Diegueño
15d. Kamia
15e. Yuma
15f. Halchidhoma and Kohuana (now Chemehuevi)
15g. Mohave

Penutian Family

Wintun
Dialect groups
16a. Northern (Wintu)
16b. Central (Nomlaki)
16c. Hill (Patwin)
16d. River (Patwin)
Maidu
Dialect groups
17a. Northeastern
17b. Northwestern
17c. Southern (Nisenan)
Miwok
18a. Coast
18b. Lake
18c. Bay (Saclan)
18d. Plains
18e. Northern Sierra
18f. Central Sierra
18g. Southern Sierra
Costanoan
19a. San Pablo (Karkin)
19b. San Francisco
19c. Santa Clara
19d. Santa Cruz
19e. San Juan Bautista (Mutsun)
19f. Rumsen (Monterey)
19g. Soledad
Yokuts
Dialect groups
20a. Northern Valley (Chulamni, Chauchila, etc.)
20b. Southern Valley (Tachi, Yauelmani, etc.)
20c. Northern Hill (Chukchansi, etc.)
20d. Kings River (Choinimni, etc.)
20e. Tule-Kaweah (Yaudanchi, etc.)
20f. Poso Creek (Paleuyami)
20g. Buena Vista (Tulamni, etc.)
Modoc
20h. Modoc

Uto-Aztekan (Shoshonean) Family

Plateau Branch
Mono-Bannock group:
21a. Northern Paiute (Paviotso)
21b. Owens Valley Paiute
21c. Mono Lake Paiute
21d. Monache (Western Mono)
Shoshoni-Comanche group:
21e. Panamint Shoshone (Koso)
Ute-Chemehuevi group:
21f. Chemehuevi (Southern Paiute)
21g. Kawaiisu (Tehachapi)
Kern River Branch
21h. Tübatulabal (and Bankalachi)
Southern California Branch
Serrano group:
21i. Kitanemuk (Tejon)
21j. Alliklik
21k. Möhineyam (Vanyume)
21l. Serrano
Gabrielino group:
21m. Fernandeño
21n. Gabrielino
21o. Nicoleño
Luiseño-Cahuilla group:
21p. Juaneño
21q. Luiseño
21r. Cupeño
21s. Pass Cahuilla
21t. Mountain Cahuilla
21u. Desert Cahuilla

	Kroeber, 1925	Powers, 1877	Handbook Amer. Inds.
Athapascan Stock	121-158	Chaps. VI-XIII	I:108-111
1a. Tolowa or Huss	121-127	65-71	II:733
Hoopa group (Hupa)	128-158	72-95	I:581-583
1b. Hoopa or Tin′–nung–hen–na′–o	128-137	72-86	I:581-583
1c. Ma′–we–nok	....	....	....
1d. 'Hwil′–kut (Whilkut)	141	88-89	II:938
1e. Tsa′–nung–wha	....	....	....
Wilakke group (Wailaki) or Nung′–hahl (Nongatl)	143, 151-158	114, 122-124	II:893-894
1f. Mat–tol′ (Mattole)	142-143	107-113	I:822-823
1g. Lo–lahn′–kok	....	113	I:773
1h. To–cho′–be	....	....	....
1i. Lassick or Ket–tel′ (Lassik)	143-144	121-122	I:761
1j. Set–ten–bi′–den	....	....	....
1k. Tsen–nah′–ken–nes	....	....	....
1l. Che–teg′–ge–kah	....	....	....
1m. Bah–ne–ko ke′–ah	....	....	....
1n. Nek′–kan–ni (Bear River)	....	....	....
1o. Kahto or To–chil–pe–ke′–ah–hahng	154-158	150-154	I:665
Polikla Stock (Yurok)	1-97	44-64	II:1012-1014
2a. Ner′–er–ner′ (Coast Yurok)	9	....	II:1013
2b. Polikla (Yurok)	8-13	....	II:1013
Soolahteluk Stock (Wiyot)			
3a. Pah′–te–wat	....	96-100	I:135
3b. We′–ke	....	101	....
3c. We′–yot	112-120	101-106	II:964-5, 967
Yukean Stock	159-168	125-138	II:1008-1009
Northwestern or Coast Division			
4a. Oo′–ko–ton–til′–kah	....	....	II:1008

	Kroeber, 1925	Powers, 1877	Handbook Amer. Inds.
Round Valley Division			
4b. Oo′–kum–nom	163, 166	126	II:865
4c. Kah′–shut–sit′–nu	. . . .	. . . .	. . . .
Upper South Eel Division			
4d. Hootch′–nom	161	136-145	I:574; II:865
4e. Wet–oo′–kum–nom	165	. . . .	II:865
4f. Tah′–too or Nar′–ko–po–mah	897	139	I:574
4g. On–kal–oo′–kum–nom (Onkolukomnom)	165	. . . .	. . . .
Southern Division (Wappo)	217-221	196-203	II:913
Mi–yahk′–mah (Makoma)	218	. . . .	I:792
4h. Mish′–a–wel band	219	196	. . . .
4i. Moo′–tis′–tool band	218	. . . .	. . . .
4j. Mi–yahk–mah band	218	. . . .	I:792
4k. Lil′–lak	. . . .	. . . .	. . . .
Lutuamean Stock	318-319	. . . .	I:778-779
5a. Mo′–dok	318-335	252-266	I:918-919
Shastan Stock	279-284	243-251	II:527-529
6a. Ko′–no–me′–ho (Konomihu)	283-284	. . . .	II:529
6b. Wah–te′–roo	. . . .	. . . .	. . . .
6c. Ke′–kahts (Kikatsik)	286	. . . .	. . . .
6d. O–kwahn′–noo–choo	284	. . . .	II:529
6c. Hah–to–ke′–he–wuk	. . . .	. . . .	?
Achomawan Stock	305-315	267-274	I:9
7a. A–choo′–mah′–we	305-315	267	I:9
7b. As–tah–ke–wi′–che (Astakiwi)	307	267	I:105-106
7c. At–wum′–we	. . . .	267	. . . .
7d. Ham–mah′–we	307	267	I:578
7e. Ha′–we–si′–doo	. . . .	. . . .	. . . .
7f. Il–mah′–we	307	267	I:600
7g. Ko–se–al–lek′–te	. . . .	. . . .	. . . .

	Kroeber, 1925	Powers, 1877	Handbook Amer. Inds.
7h. Mo–des′–se (Mahdesi)	307	....	....
7i. To–mal–lin′–che–moi′	....	....	....
7j. At–soo–ka′–e (Atsugewi)	315	267	1:113-114
7k. Ap–woo′–ro–ka′–e	....	....	....
7l. A–me′–che	....	....	....
7m. E–poo′–de	....	....	....
Karok Stock	98-108	19-43	I:659; II:347
8a. Ar′–rahr	....	....	I:659
8b. Kah–rah′–ko–hah (Karok)	98-108	19	I:659
Tlohomtahhoi Stock			
9a. Tlo′–hom–tah′–hoi (New River Shasta)	282-283	91	....
Chemareko Stock	109-112	92-95	
10a. Chemareko	109-112	92-95	I:270
Yahnah Stock	336-346	275-281	II:987-988
11a. Yah′–nah	336-341	....	II:987
Pomo Stock	222-271	146	II:276-277
Northern Division or Family			
12a. Mah′–to–po′–mah	230, 238	....	....
12b. Me–tum′–mah	....	155	....
12c. Kah′–be–tsim′–me–po′–mah	....	....	....
12d. Po–mo′–ke–chah′	....	....	....
12e. Mah–soo′–tah–ke′–ah (Masut)	230	....	I:818
12f. Mah–too′–go	....	....	....
12g. Ki–yow′–bah[ch] (Kaiyau)	231	....	....
Yokiah–Boyah Division	....		
12h. Boyah	....	....	....
12i. Tah′–bah–ta′	231		II:277

	Kroeber, 1925	Powers, 1877	Handbook Amer. Inds.
12j. Lah'–ta	232	. . . .	. . . .
12k. Kan–no'–ah	. . . .	. . . .	. . . .
12l. Yo–ki'–ah	232	163-167	II:277, 999
12m. She–a'–ko (Shiego)	232	. . . .	II:277
12n. Sho–ko'–ah or Sha–nel	230, 232	168-173	II:553
12o. Den–nol'–yo–keah	231	. . . .	. . . .
12p. Yo–buk'–ka'–ah (Yobutui)	231	. . . .	II:277
Kah–chi'–ah Division	. . . .	. . . .	. . . .
12q. Kah–chi–ah	. . . .	. . . .	. . . .
Mah'–kah–mo–chum'–mi or We–shum'–tat–tah Division		. . . .	. . . .
12r. Mah'–kah–mo–chum'–mi	233		. . . .
12s. Shah–kow'–we–chum'–mi	233	. . . .	. . . .
12t. We'–shah'–chum'–mi	. . . .	. . . .	. . . .
12u. Me–hin–kow'–nah	. . . .	. . . .	. . . .
12v. We–shum'–tat–tah	. . . .	. . . .	. . . .
Han–nah'–bah–[ch] or Clear Lake Division			
12w. Dan–no'–kah	231	. . . .	I:382
12x. She'–kum (Shigom)	231, 238	. . . .	II:547
12y. Bo–al–ke'–ah	231	155	II:277
12z. Ku'–lan–na'–po	228		I:732
12aa. Ha'–be–nap'–po (Khabenapo)	220	205	I:677
Sho–te'–ah or Stony Creek Division			
12bb. Sho–te'–ah (Cheetido)	232	. . . .	. . . .
Ham–fo or Lower Lake Division			
12cc. Ham'–fo (Anạmfo)	228	. . . .	. . . .
Chumash Stock	550-568	. . . .	I:296-297
13a. Ah'–moo	. . . .	. . . .	. . . .

	Kroeber, 1925	Powers, 1877	Handbook Amer. Inds.
13b. Kah′–she–nahs–moo	....	....	....
13c. Kah′–sah–kom–pe′–ah	....	....	....
13d. Kas′–swah (Cashwah)	....	....	I:211-212
13e. Chu–mahs	550-568		I:296-297
13f. Hool′–koo–koo	....	....	....
13g. Tso–yin′–ne–ah–koo	....	....	....
Yuman Stock	709-803	....	II:1011-1012
14a. Mohave	726-780	....	I:919-921
14b. Kam′–me–i	723-725	....	I:390
14c. Tis–se′–pah	....	....	....
14d. Yu′–man	709-723	....	I:390
14e. Diegueño	....	....	....
14f. Es–kah′–ti			
Washoo Stock			
15a. Washoo	568-573	....	II:920
Esselen Stock	544-546	....	I:438
16a. Esselen	544-546	....	I:438
Ennesen Stock (Salinan)	546-549	....	II:415
17a. Antoniano or Kah–tri–tam (?)	....	568	....
17b. Migueleño or Te–po–trahl (?)	....	....	....
17c. Lahm–kah–trahm (?)	....	....	....
Olhonean Stock (Costanoan)	462-473	....	I:351; II:118-9
18a. Hor–de–on	....	....	....
18b. Hoo′–mon–twash	....	....	....
18c. Moot–soon′	444, 463	....	1:351
18d. Achestah	....	....	....
18e. Kah′–koon or Room–se–en	....	....	....
18f. Yak′–shoon	....	....	....

	Kroeber, 1925	Powers, 1877	Handbook Amer. Inds.
Wintoon Stock	347-363	229-242	II:963
Northern Wintoon	....	229	....
19a. Wintu or Num′–soos Wintoon	352, 355	....	....
19b. Num′–te–pom′ or Wintoon proper	354	229	II:343
19c. Nor′–rel–muk (Normuk)	356	230, 231	II:83
19d. Ni–i′–che	....	....	....
19e. Daw′–pum	356	....	....
Nom–lak–ke or Central Division		....	
19f. Nom′–lak–ke	356	230	II:79
19g. Wi–e′–ker′–ril band	....	....	....
19h. Dah′–chin–chin′–ne	....	....	....
19i. Te–ha′–mah	897	....	II:79
19j. No–e–muk (Norelmuk?)	356	231	II:83
19k. No–mel′–te–ke′–we (Nomecult?)	896	230	....
Southern Division (Patwin)	354	218-228	II:211
19l. Choo–hel′–mem–shel	....	....	....
19m. Chen′–po–sel	356	219	I:343
19n. Lol′–sel band	356	219	I:343
19o. Klet′–win	....	....	....
19p. Ko–pa or Win (Copeh)	355	....	I:343
19q. Nan′–noo–ta′–we or Nap′–pa	356	218	II:27
19r. Ko′–roo (Korusi)	....	219	I:727
19s. Pat′–win	355	219	I:343
19t. Poo′–e–win	....	....	....
Midoo Stock	391-441	282-345	I:326-327
Northern Division	....	....	I:790
20a. Mitchopdo	394	282	I:858
20b. No′–to–koi′–yu	....	....	....
20c. Sa–ap–kahn–ko band	....	....	....
20d. Nah′–kahn–ko band	....	315	....

	Kroeber, 1925	Powers, 1877	Handbook Amer. Inds.
20e. O–so′–ko band	....	....	....
Central Division			
20f. Kon′–kow or Ti′–mah (Concow)	895	283, 313	I:725, 790
20g. Tahn′–kum (Tankum)	394	....	II:75
20h. Kow′–wahk	....	....	....
20i. Kum–mo′–win	....	....	....
Southern Division or Nissenan	445	313-345	II:75
20j. To–sim′–me–nan	....	....	....
20k. Ho′–mah band	....	....	....
20l. Nis′–sim Pa′–we–nan	....	....	....
20m. Nis′–se–nan′	392	313-345	II:75
20n. No–to′–mus′–se band	....	....	....
20o. Es′–to Nis′–se–nan band	....	....	....
Mewan Stock (Miwok)	442-461	356-368	I:941-942
Me–wuk or Sierra tribes (3 divisions)	442-445		....
21a. Northern Me′–wuk	445	347	....
21b. Hoo–ka–go band	....	....	....
21c. Middle Me′–wuk	445	347	....
21d. Southern Me′–wuk	445	347	....
21e. Po–ho′–ne–che band	443	350	II:272
Mew–ko or Plains tribes			
21f. Hul–pom′–ne (Hulpumni)	444	....	I:680
21g. Mo–koz′–um–ne (Mokosumni)	444	347	I:352
21h. O′–che–hak (Ochehamni?)	444-445	....	....
21i. Wi′–pa (Guaypem; Khulpuni)	445	....	I:680
21j. Han–ne′–suk	....	....	....
21k. Yatch–a–chum′–ne (Yachikamne)	485	....	II:982

	Kroeber, 1925	Powers, 1877	Handbook Amer. Inds.
21l. Mo–kal′–um–ne (Mokelumni)	444-445	347	I:930
21m. Chil–um′–ne	....	....	....
21n. Si′–a–kum′–ne (Sakayakumne)	444	....	....
21o. Tu–ol′–um–ne	897	....	II:839
21p. Saclan	463	....	II:402
In–ne–ko tribes (Coast Miwok)		....	II:941
21q. Tu′–le–yo′–me	272	....	....
21r. Hoo′–koo–e′–ko	273	....	....
21s. Olamentko	273	537	II:118
21t. Le–kah′–te–wuk (Likatuit)	273	195	....
Yokut Stock	474-491	369-392	I:807-808
22a. Heu′–che	484	....	I:808
22b. Chow–chil′–lah	484	....	I:292
22c. Chuck–chan′–sy	481	370	I:295
22d. To–ko′–lo band (?) (Toholo)	484	....	....
22e. Tal–lin′–che (Dalinchi)	481	....	II:678
22f. Pit–kah′–che	484	370	II:265
22g. Toom′–nah band (Dumna)	481	....	II:837
22h. Ketch–a′–ye	481	....	I:670
22i. Kum′–nah	....	....	....
22j. Kosh–sho′–o or Ko–sho–o or Ko–shon (Kassoyo, Gashowu?	481	370	I:663
22k. Ho–ye′–mah	484	....	....
22l. Chu–ki′–ah	....	....	....
22m. Cho–e–nim′–ne	480	370	I:290
22n. Wa′–cha–kut (Wechikit?)	....	370	II:929
22o. Cho–ki′–min–nah (Chukamina)	480	370	....

	Kroeber, 1925	Powers, 1877	Handbook Amer. Inds.
22p. No–to′–no–to (Nutunutu)	483	370	II:100
22q. Tah′–che	483	370	II:667
22r. Wik–chum′–ne	480	393	II:952
22s. Ka–we′–ahs (Kawia)	480	370	I:668-669
22t. Ta–dum′–ne (Telamni)	....	....	II:726
22u. Choo′–nut	483	370	I:298
22v. Choi′–nook or Cho′–nook or Choo′–enu or Wa–da′–she	482	....	I:290
22w. Yo′–kol or Yo–o′–kul or Yo′–a–kud′–dy	....	370	II:999
22x. Yow–lan′–che (Yaulanchi)	479	....	II:994
22y. No–chan′–itch band	....	....	....
22z. Ko–yet′–te	482	....	I:729
22aa. Pal–low′–yam′–me (Paleuyami)	479	....	II:193
22bb. Wo′–wul (Wolasi)	482	....	II:968
22cc. Yow′–el–man′–ne (Yaulmani)	482	....	II:994
22dd. Tin′–lin–ne (Tinlinin)	482	370	....
22ee. Too–lol′–min	....	....	....
22ff. Ye–wum′–ne or Pah–ah′–se	....	....	....
22gg. Ham–met–wel′–le (Hometwoli)	478	....	....
22hh. Tu–lum′–ne (Telamni?)	482	370	....
Shoshone Stock	574-580	....	II:555-558
23a. Northern Piute			
23b. Koo–tsab′–be dik′–ka	....	....	....

	Kroeber, 1925	Powers, 1877	Handbook Amer. Inds.
23c. Pahng′–we–hoo′–tse	....	....	....
Monache Piute			
Western Monache	580	396-399	I:932
23d. Nim or Monache	896	....	
23e. Posh–ge′–sha	585	....	II:288
23f. Kwe′–tah	....	....	....
23g. Too–hook′–mutch	....	....	....
23h. Ko–ko–he′–ba band	585	....	....
23i. Toi–ne′–che band (Toihicha, Talinchi)	480	....	II:678
23j. Hol′–ko–mah band	585		I:557
23k. To–win–che′–ba band	585	....	I:557
23l. Wo′–pon–nutch	585	....	....
23m. En′–tim–bitch	480, 585	....	I:611
23n. Wuksä–che′ (Waksachi)	586	....	II:898
23o. Pot–wish′–ah (Balwisha)	586	....	I:124
Owens Lake Monache Piute	....	397	I:932
23p. Kwe′–nah–pat′–se band	....	....	....
23q. Ut′–te–ur–re–we′–te	....	....	....
23r. To′–bo–ah–hax-ze	....	....	....
23s. Chuk′–ke–sher–ra′–ka	....	....	....
23t. No′–no–pi–ah	....	....	....
Panamints	589-592	....	II:199
23u. Pak′–wa–sitch	....	....	....
23v. Moo–et′–tah (Muah?)	896	....	....
Southern Piute			
23w. New–oo′–ah (Kawaiisu)	601-605	393	I:666
23x. Tol–chin′–ne	....	....	....
23y. Nu–vah′–an–dits	....	....	....
23z. Chem–e–we′–ve′	593-600	....	I:242-243
Ke–tahn–na–mwits or Serrano	595, 611-613	....	II:512-513

	Kroeber, 1925	Powers, 1877	Handbook Amer. Inds.
23aa. Ke–tah′–na′–mwits (Kitanemuk)	....	....	....
23bb. Pur′–ve′–tum or Pur–vit–tem	....	....	....
23cc. Yo–hah′–ve–tum	....	....	....
23dd. Mah′–re–ah–ne–um or Mah′–ring–i–um or Mo′–he–ah′–ne–um	616	....	II:513
Kah-we-sik-tem or Cahuilla	692-708	....	I:668-669
23ee. Koos′–tam	....	....	....
23ff. Wah′–ne–ke′–tam or Mahl′–ke	....	....	....
23gg. Kah–we–sik′–tem	....	....	....
23hh. Pan′–yik–tem	....	....	....
23ii. Wah–ko–chim′–kut–tem	....	....	....
23jj. Sow′–wis–pah–kik′–tem	....	....	....
23kk. Pow′–we–yam	....	....	....
23ll. We–is′–tem		....	....
Koo′–pah			
23mm. Koo′–pah	689	....	....
A–katch′–mah or Luiseno	648-688	....	I:777-778
23nn. A–katch′–mah	636	....	....
23oo. Pi–yum′–ko	....	....	....
23pp. So–bo′–ba	896	....	II:400-401
Tongva Stock			
24a. Tongva (Gabrielino)	620-633	....	I:480
Tubotelobela Stock	....	393	....
25a. Pahn′–ka–la′–che (Bankalachi)	607	....	II:830
25b. Tu′–bot–e–lob′–e–la (Tubatulabal)	605-610	....	II:830

BIBLIOGRAPHY

BIBLIOGRAPHY

Aginsky, B. W.

1943 Culture element distributions: XXIV, Central Sierra. University of California Publications: Anthropological Records, Vol. 8, No. 4.

Arroyo de la Cuesta, F.

1861 Grammar of the Mutsun language. Shea's Library of American Linguistics. Vol. 4. New York.

1862 Vocabulary of the Mutsun language. Shea's Library of American Linguistics. Vol. 8. New York.

Barrett, S. A.

1908 The ethnogeography of the Pomo and neighboring Indians. University of California Publications in American Archaeology and Ethnology, Vol. 6, No. 1.

1908 The geography and dialects of the Miwok Indians. University of California Publications in American Archaeology and Ethnology, Vol. 6:333–368.

1917 The Washo Indians. Bulletin of the Public Museum of the City of Milwaukee, Vol. 2:1–52.

1952 Material aspects of Pomo culture. Part I. Bulletin of the Public Museum of the City of Milwaukee, Vol. 20, No. 1.

Baumhoff, M. A.

1958 California Athabascan groups. University of California Publications: Anthropological Records, Vol. 16, No. 5.

Baumhoff, M. A., and D. L. Olmsted

1964 Notes on Palaihnihan culture history: Glottochronology and Archaeology. University of California Publications in Linguistics, Vol. 34:1–12.

Beals, Ralph L.

1933 Ethnology of the Nisenan. University of California Publications in American Archaeology and Ethnology, Vol. 31, No. 6.

Beeler, M. S.

1955 Saclan. International Journal of American Linguistics, Vol. 21:201–209.

1959 Saclan once more. International Journal of American Linguistics, Vol. 25:67–68.

Benedict, R. F.

1924 A brief sketch of Serrano culture. American Anthropologist, Vol. 26:366–392.

Bennyhoff, J. A.
n. d. The ethnogeography of the Plains Miwok. Doctoral dissertation (unpublished), University of California (Berkeley).

Bonnerjea, B.
1963 Index to Bulletins 1–100 of the Bureau of American Ethnology. Bureau of American Ethnology, Bulletin 178.

Bright, W., ed.
1964 Studies in California linguistics. University of California Publications in Linguistics, Vol. 34.

Brinton, D. G.
1901 The American race. David McKay Co., Philadelphia.

Broadbent, S. M.
1957 Rumsen I: Methods of reconstruction. International Journal of American Linguistics, Vol. 23:275–280.

Bruff, J. G.
1949 The journals, drawings and other papers of J. Goldsborough Bruff. Edited by G. W. Read and R. Gaines. 2 vols. Columbia University Press, New York.

Callaghan, C. A.
1964 Phonemic borrowing in Lake Miwok. University of California Publications in Linguistics, Vol. 34:46–53.

Chamberlain, A. F.
1910 Linguistic families. Bureau of American Ethnology, Bulletin 30, Vol. 1:766–768.

Collins, C. R.
1876 Report on the languages of the different tribes of Indians inhabiting the territory of Utah. Appendix P in J. H. Simpson, Report of explorations across the great basin of the territory of Utah . . . in 1859. Washington, D. C.

Cook, S. F.
1955 The aboriginal population of the San Joaquin Valley, California. University of California Publications: Anthropological Records, Vol. 16:31–80.
1956 The aboriginal population of the North Coast of California. University of California Publications: Anthropological Records, Vol. 16, No. 3.
1957 The aboriginal population of Alameda and Contra Costa Counties, California. University of California Publications: Anthropological Records, Vol. 16, No. 4.

Curtis, E. S.
1924 The North American Indian. Vol. 13. Norwood, Massachusetts.

Cutter, D. C.
1960 The California Franciscans as anthropologists. Southwest Museum Masterkey, Vol. 34:88–94.

Davis, L. B.
1963 The development of native North American linguistic taxonomy (1600–1958). Dept. of Sociology, Anthropology and Social Welfare, Montana State University. Anthropology and Sociology Papers, No. 26.

De Angulo, Jaime, and L. S. Freeland
1929 Notes on the Northern Paiute of California. Journal de la Société des Americanistes de Paris, Nouvelle Série, Vol. 21:313–335.

Dixon, Roland B.
1905 The Northern Maidu. Bulletin of the American Museum of Natural History, Vol. 17, No. 3:119–346.
1905 The Shasta-Achomawi: a new linguistic stock with four new dialects. American Anthropologist, N. S., Vol. 7:213–217.
1907 Linguistic relationships within the Shasta-Achomawi stock. International Congress of Americanists, XV Session, Vol. 2:255–263.
1907 The Shasta. Bulletin of the American Museum of Natural History, Vol. 17, No. 5:381–498.

Dixon, R. B., and A. L. Kroeber
1913 New linguistic families in California. American Anthropologist, Vol. 15:647–655.
1919 Linguistic families of California. University of California Publications in American Archaeology and Ethnology, Vol. 16:47–118.

Driver, Harold E.
1936 Wappo ethnography. University of California Publications in American Archaeology and Ethnology, Vol. 36, No. 3.
1937 Culture element distributions: VI, Southern Sierra Nevada. University of California Publications: Anthropological Records, Vol. 1, No. 2.
1939 Culture element distributions: X, Northwest California. University of California Publications: Anthropological Records, Vol. 1, No. 6.
1961 Indians of North America. University of Chicago Press, Chicago.

Drucker, Philip
1937 The Tolowa and their Southwest Oregon kin. University of California Publications in American Archaeology and Ethnology, Vol. 36, No. 4.

DuBois, Cora
1935 Wintu ethnography. University of California Publications in American Archaeology and Ethnology, Vol. 36, No. 1.

Essene, Frank
1942 Culture element distribution: XXI, Round Valley. University of California Publications: Anthropological Records, Vol. 8, No. 1.

Fages, Pedro
1937 A historical, political and natural description of California. Translated by H. I. Priestley. University of California Press, Berkeley.

Forde, C. Daryll
1931 Ethnography of the Yuma Indians. University of California Publications in American Archaeology and Ethnology, Vol. 28, No. 4.

Foster, George M.
1944 A summary of Yuki culture. University of California Publications: Anthropological Records, Vol. 5, No. 3.

Garth, Thomas R.
1953 Atsugewi ethnography. University of California Publications: Anthropological Records, Vol. 14, No. 2.

Gatschet, A. S.
1876*a* Eleven idioms of Southern California. Report to the Secretary of War for 1876. Part 3: Report to the Chief of Engineers, pp. 550–563.
1876*b* Zwolf Sprachen aus dem Südwesten Nordamerikas. Hermann Bohlau, Weimar.
1877 Indian languages of the Pacific States and Territories. Magazine of American History (New York), Vol. 1:145–171.
1877–1886 Der Yuma-Sprachstamm. Zeitschrift für Ethnologie, Vol. 10:341–350, 366–418 (1877); Vol. 15:123–147 (1883); Vol. 18:97–122 (1886).
1882 Indian languages of the Pacific states and territories and of the Pueblos of New Mexico. Magazine of American History, Vol. 8:254–263.

Gayton, A. H.
1948 Yokuts and Western Mono ethnography. University of California Publications: Anthropological Records, Vol. 10, Nos. 1 and 2.

Geiger, M., ed.
1949 Questionnaire of the Spanish government in 1812 concerning the native culture of the California Mission Indians. The Americas, Vol. 5, No. 4:474–490.
1950 Reply to Mission San Carlos Borromeo to the questionnaire of the Spanish government in 1812 concerning the native culture of the California Mission Indians. The Americas, Vol. 6, No. 4:467–486.

Gifford, E. W.
1918 Clans and moieties in Southern California. University of California Publications in American Archaeology and Ethnology, Vol. 14, No. 2.

1923 Pomo lands on Clear Lake. University of California Publications in American Archaeology and Ethnology, Vol. 20:70–92.

1931 The Kamia of Imperial Valley. Bureau of American Ethnology, Bulletin 97.

1932 The Northfork Mono. University of California Publications in American Archaeology and Ethnology, Vol. 31, No. 2.

1939 The Coast Yuki. Anthropos, Vol. 34:292–375.

Gifford, Edward W., and Stanislaw Klimek

1936 Culture element distributions: II, Yana. University of California Publications in American Archaeology and Ethnology, Vol. 37, No. 2.

Gifford, Edward W., and Alfred L. Kroeber

1937 Culture element distributions: IV, Pomo. University of California Publications in American Archaeology and Ethnology, Vol. 37, No. 4.

Goddard, P. E.

1914 The present condition of our knowledge of North American languages. American Anthropologist, Vol. 16:555–601.

1914 Notes on the Chilula Indians of Northwestern California. University of California Publications in American Archaeology and Ethnology, Vol. 10:265–288.

1923 The habitat of the Wailaki. University of California Publications in American Archaeology and Ethnology, Vol. 20:95–109.

Goldschmidt, Walter

1951 Nomlaki ethnography. University of California Publications in American Archaeology and Ethnology, Vol. 42:303–443.

Haas, Mary

1958 Algonkian-Ritwan: the end of a controversy. International Journal of Linguistics, Vol. 24:159–173.

Hale, H.

1846 Ethnology and philology. U.S. exploring expedition during the years 1838–1842 under the command of Charles Wilkes, U.S.N. Vol. 6. Philadelphia.

Hardacre, E. C.

1880 Eighteen years alone. Scribners Monthly, Vol. 20:657–664.

Hayden, H. E.

1877 Indian languages of the Pacific. Magazine of American History, Vol. 1:331.

Heizer, R. F.

1941 Alexander S. Taylor's map of California Indian tribes, 1864. California Historical Society Quarterly, Vol. 20:171–180.

1942 Archaeological evidence of Sebastian Rodriguez Cermeño's California visit of 1595. California Historical Society Quarterly, Vol. 20:315–328.

1947 Francis Drake and the California Indians, 1579. University of California Publications in American Archaeology and Ethnology, Vol. 42:251–302.

1952 California Indian linguistic records: the Mission Indian vocabularies of Alphonse Pinart. University of California Publications: Anthropological Records, Vol. 15, No. 1.

1955 California Indian linguistic records: the Mission Indian vocabularies of H. W. Henshaw. University of California Publications: Anthropological Records, Vol. 15, No. 2.

1958 Aboriginal California and Great Basin cartography. University of California Archaeological Survey, Report No. 41:1–9.

Heizer, R. F., and W. W. Elmendorf

1942 Francis Drake's California anchorage in the light of the Indian language spoken there. Pacific Historical Review, Vol. 11:213–217.

Heizer, R. F., and A. B. Elsasser

1963 Original accounts of the lone woman of San Nicolas Island. University of California Archaeological Survey, Report No. 55.

Heizer, R. F., and M. A. Whipple

1951 The California Indians, a source book. University of California Press, Berkeley.

Henshaw, H. W.

1890 A new linguistic family in California. American Anthropologist, O.S., Vol. 3:45–49.

Hewes, M. and G.

1952 Indian life and customs at Mission San Luis Rey. The Americas, Vol. 9:87–106.

Hodge, F. W., ed.

1907 Handbook of American Indians. Part I, A-M. Bureau of American Ethnology, Bulletin 30.

1910 Handbook of American Indians. Part II, N-Z. Bureau of American Ethnology, Bulletin 30.

Hoijer, H.

1941 Methods in the classification of American Indian languages. *In* Language, culture and personality, ed. by L. Spier, A. Hallowell, and S. Newman. Menasha, Wisconsin. pp. 3–14.

Hoijer, H., *et al.*

1946 Linguistic structures of native America. Viking Fund Publications in Anthropology, No. 6. New York.

Holt, Catherine

1946 Shasta ethnography. University of California Publications: Anthropological Records, Vol. 3, No. 4.

Hooper, Lucile
1920 The Cahuilla Indians. University of California Publications in American Archaeology and Ethnology, Vol. 16, No. 6.

Hymes, D. H.
1961 Kroeber, Powell and Henshaw. Anthropological Linguistics, Vol. 3:15–16.

Jacobs, M.
1930 A sketch of Northern Sahaptin grammar. University of Washington Publications in Anthropology, Vol. 4. Seattle.

Johnston, A.
1854 Languages of California. *In* H. Schoolcraft, Indian tribes of the United States, Vol. 4:406–415.

Jones, S. J.
1961 Some regional aspects of native California. Scottish Geographical Magazine 67:19–30.

Kelly, Isabel T.
1932 Ethnography of the Surprise Valley Paiute. University of California Publications in American Archaeology and Ethnology, Vol. 31, No. 3.

Kniffen, Fred B.
1928 Achomawi geography. University of California Publications in American Archaeology and Ethnology, Vol. 23, No. 5:297–332.
1939 Pomo geography. University of California Publications in American Archaeology and Ethnology, Vol. 36:353–400.

Kroeber, A. L.
1904 The languages of the coast of California south of San Francisco. University of California Publications in American Archaeology and Ethnology, Vol. 2, No. 2.
1907 Shoshonean dialects of California. University of California Publications in American Archaeology and Ethnology, Vol. 4, No. 3.
1908*a* On the evidences of the occupation of certain regions by Miwok Indians. University of California Publications in American Archaeology and Ethnology, Vol. 6:369–380.
1908*b* A mission record of the California Indians: from a manuscript in the Bancroft Library. University of California Publications in American Archaeology and Ethnology, Vol. 8:1–27.
1908*c* The anthropology of California. Science, N.S., 27:281–290. (Reprinted, 1962, with notes by D. Hymes and R. F. Heizer, in University of California Archaeological Survey, Report No. 56:1–18.)
1910 The Chumash and Costanoan languages. University of California Publications in American Archaeology and Ethnology, Vol. 9, No. 2.
1920 Yuman tribes of the Lower Colorado River. University of California Publications in American Archaeology and Ethnology, Vol. 16, No. 8.

1925 Handbook of the Indians of California. Bureau of American Ethnology, Bulletin 78.

1932 The Patwin and their neighbors. University of California Publications in Archaeology and Ethnology, Vol. 29:253–423.

1936 Preface to Culture element distributions: II, Yana. University of California Publications in American Archaeology and Ethnology, Vol. 37:71–74.

1939 Cultural and natural areas of native North America. University of California Press, Berkeley. Reprinted in 1963. Originally published in University of California Publications in Amercan Archaeology and Ethnology, Vol. 38.

1940 Conclusions: the present status of Americanistic problems. *In* C. L. Hay, *et al.*, eds. The Maya and their neighbors. Appleton-Century, New York. pp. 460–487.

1951 A Mohave historical epic. University of California Publications: Anthropological Records, Vol. 11, No. 2.

1955*a* C. Hart Merriam as anthropologist. *In* C. Hart Merriam, Studies of California Indians. University of California Press, Berkeley. pp. vii–xiv.

1955*b* Nature of the land-holding group. Ethnohistory, Vol. 2:303–314.

1957 Some new group boundaries in Central California. University of California Publications in American Archaeology and Ethnology, Vol. 47:215–217.

1959 Ethnographic interpretations, 7–11. University of California Publications in American Archaeology and Ethnology, Vol. 47, No. 3.

1960 Powell and Henshaw: an episode in the history of ethnolinguistics. Anthropological Linguistics, Vol. 2:1–5.

1962 The anthropology of California. Annotated by D. W. Hymes and R. F. Heizer. University of California Archaeological Survey, Report No. 56:1–18.

Kroeber, A. L., and G. W. Grace

1960 The Sparkman grammar of Luiseño. University of California Publications in Linguistics, Vol. 16.

Latham, Robert Gordon

1854 On the languages of New California. Proceedings of the Philological Society of London for 1852 and 1853, Vol. 6:72–86.

1856 On the languages of Northern, Western and Central America. Transactions of the Philological Society of London, 1856, pp. 57–115.

Loeb, Edwin M.

1926 Pomo folkways. University of California Publications in American Archaeology and Ethnology, Vol. 19, No. 2.

1932 The western Kuksu cult. University of California Publications in American Archaeology and Ethnology, Vol. 33, No. 1.

Longinos, Jose Martinez

1938 California in 1792. The expedition of Jose Longinos Martinez. Translated by Lesley Byrd Simpson. Huntington Library Publications, San Marino.

1961 Journal of Jose Longinos Martinez. Translated and edited by Lesley Byrd Simpson. John Howell Books, San Francisco.

Loud, L. L.

1918 Ethnogeography and archaeology of the Wiyot territory, University of California Publications in American Archaeology and Ethnology, Vol. 14, No. 2.

Mason, J. A.

1916 The Mutsun dialect of Costanoan based on the vocabulary of de la Cuesta. University of California Publications in American Archaeology and Ethnology, Vol. 9:399–472.

Merriam, C. Hart

1926 The classification and distribution of the Pit River Indian tribes of California. Smithsonian Miscellaneous Collections, Vol. 78, No. 3.

1930 The New River Indians, Tlo–hom′–tah–hoi′. American Anthropologist, Vol. 32:280–292.

1955 Studies of California Indians. University of California Press, Berkeley.

Michelson, T. H.

1914 The alleged Algonquian languages of California. American Anthropologist, N.S., Vol. 16:361–367.

Murdock, G. P.

1960 Ethnographic bibliography of North America. 3d ed. Behavior Science Monographs, Human Relations Area Files, New Haven, Connecticut.

Nomland, G. A.

1935 Sinkyone notes. University of California Publications in American Archaeology and Ethnology, Vol. 36, No. 2.

1938 Bear River ethnography. University of California Publications: Anthropological Records, Vol. 2, No. 2.

Park, W. Z.

1938 Tribal distribution in the Great Basin. American Anthropologist, Vol. 40:622–638.

Powers, Stephen

1877 Tribes of California. Contributions to North American Ethnology, Vol. 3. Washington, D. C.

Price, John A.
1962 Washo economy. Nevada State Museum Anthropological Papers, No. 6.

Redfield, R.
1955 The little community: viewpoints for the study of a human whole. University of Chicago Press, Chicago.

Sapir, E.
1913 Wiyot and Yurok, Algonkin languages of California. American Anthropologist, Vol. 15:617–646.

Sapir, E., and L. Spier
1941 Notes on the culture of the Yana. University of California Publications: Anthropological Records, Vol. 3, No. 3.

Schenck, W. E.
1926 Historic aboriginal groups of the California Delta region. University of California Publications in American Archaeology and Ethnology, Vol. 23, No. 2.

Schoolcraft, Henry
1853 Language. Part III of Indian tribes of the United States, pp. 397–460. Philadelphia.

Scouler, J.
1841 Observations on the indigenous tribes of the northeast coast of America. Journal of the Royal Geographical Society, Vol. 11: 215–251.

Sitjar, B.
1861 Vocabulary of the language of San Antonio Mission, California. Shea's Library of American Linguistics, Vol. 7. New York.

Spencer, R. F., J. D. Jennings, *et al.*
1965 The native Americans. Harper and Row, New York.

Spier, Leslie
1923 Southern Diegueño customs. University of California Publications in American Archaeology and Ethnology, Vol. 20:297-358.
1933 Yuman tribes of the Colorado River. University of Chicago Press, Chicago.

Spott, Robert, and A. L. Kroeber
1942 Yurok narratives. University of California Publications in American Archaeology and Ethnology, Vol. 35, No. 9.

Steward, J. H.
1933 Ethnography of the Owens Valley Paiute. University of California Publications in American Archaeology and Ethnology, Vol. 33: 233–350.

1937 Linguistic distributions and political groups of the Great Basin Shoshoneans. American Anthropologist, Vol. 39:625–634.

1938 Basin-Plateau aboriginal socio-political groups. Bureau of American Ethnology, Bulletin 120.

Stewart, George W.

1927 The Yokut Indians of the Kaweah region. Sierra Club Bulletin, Vol. 12, No. 4.

Stewart, Omer C.

1943 Notes on Pomo ethnogeography. University of California Publications in American Archaeology and Ethnology, Vol. 40, No. 2.

1961 Kroeber and the Indian Claims Commission cases. Kroeber Anthropological Society, Paper No. 25:181–190.

Strong, William D.

1929 Aboriginal society in Southern California. University of California Publications in American Archaeology and Ethnology, Vol. 26.

Sturtevant, W.

1959 Authorship of the Powell linguistic classification. International Journal of American Linguistics, Vol. 25:196–199.

Swanton, J. R.

1952 The Indian tribes of North America. Bureau of American Ethnology, Bulletin 145.

Taylor, A. S.

1860–1863 Indianology of California. California Farmer and Journal of Useful Sciences, Vols. 13-20.

Taylor, E. G. R.

1932 Francis Drake and the Pacific: two fragments. Pacific Historical Review, Vol. 1:360–369.

Thompson, Lucy

1916 To the American Indian. Eureka, California.

Thompson, T. H., and A. A. West

1883 History of Santa Barbara County. Oakland.

Trager, G. L., and F. E. Harben

1958 North American Indian languages: classification and maps. Studies in Linguistics, No. 5.

Turner, W. W.

1856 Report upon the Indian tribes, by Lt. A. W. Whipple, Thomas Ewbank, and W. W. Turner. Pacific Railroad, Reports of Explorations and Surveys, Vol. 3, Part 3.

Voegelin, C. F.

1941 North American Indian languages still spoken and their genetic relationships. *In* Language, culture, and personality, ed. by L. Spier, A. Hallowell, and S. Newman, Menasha, Wisconsin. pp. 15–40.

Voegelin, E. W.

1938 Tubatulabal ethnography. University of California Publications: Anthropological Records, Vol. 2, No. 1.

1942 Culture element distributions: XX, Northeast California. University of California Publications: Anthropological Records, Vol. 7, No. 2.

Wagner, H. R.

1924 The voyage to California of Sebastian Rodriguez Cermeno in 1595. California Historical Society Quarterly, Vol. 3:3–24.

1926 Sir Francis Drake's voyage around the world. San Francisco.

1928 Spanish voyages to the northeast coast in the sixteenth century. Chapter 4: The voyage of Juan Rodriguez Cabrillo. California Historical Society Quarterly, Vol. 8, No. 1:20–77.

Wallace, W. J.

1949 Hupa warfare. Southwest Museum Leaflets, No. 23.

Waterman, T. T.

1920 Yurok geography. University of California Publications in American Archaeology and Ethnology, Vol. 16, No. 5.

1925 Village sites in Tolowa and neighboring areas of Northwestern California. American Anthropologist, Vol. 27:528–543.

Wheeler-Voegelin, E.

1956 History and ethnohistory, and a case in point. *In* Men and cultures, ed. by A. F. C. Wallace. Selected Papers of the Fifth International Congress of Anthropological and Ethnological Sciences. University of Pennsylvania Press, Philadelphia.